LATIN@ IDENTITY IN PNEUMATOLOGICAL PERSPECTIVE
MESTIZAJE AND *HIBRIDEZ*

Latin@ Identity in Pneumatological Perspective

Mestizaje and Hibridez

Daniel Orlando Álvarez

CPT Press
Cleveland, Tennessee

Latin@ Identity in Pneumatological Perspective
Mestizaje and *Hibridez*

Published by CPT Press
900 Walker ST NE
Cleveland, TN 37311
USA
email: cptpress@pentecostaltheology.org
website: www.cptpress.com

Library of Congress Control Number: 2016951006
ISBN-13: 978-1-935931-59-1

For my wife

Rachel,

who has shown me love, compassion, and understanding.

TABLE OF CONTENTS

ACKNOWLEDGEMENTS

I want to acknowledge and thank the many individuals and communities that were a valuable part of this journey. Dale Coulter, demonstrated sincere interest during a critical part of my journey at Regent. His interest, advice, and input encouraged me to pursue this topic for my dissertation. I also wish to thank the dissertation committee members, Néstor Medina, who came along at a critical juncture, and Arlene Sánchez Walsh. The idea for this topic was birthed in a class with Stan Burgess. I wish to acknowledge Eric Newberg as the person who constantly thought of my doctoral cohort. He kept us together and was a guiding light throughout this arduous process.

From my community in New York, I thank the members of the Staten Island Church of God for their support and patience as I finished this project. I also wish to recognize the hundreds of undocumented immigrants whose hard work and labor goes unnoticed. They inspired me to value every human being and to strive for a better future through education. Many of them are committed Christians in Pentecostal churches.

I wish to recognize my family and extended family for being there for me always. I have not forgotten where I came from. Finally, I wish to thank my wife, Rachel. I could have never done this without her. *Te quiero mucho.*

1

UNDERSTANDING LATIN@S[1] IN THE UNITED STATES

Introduction

Our world is quickly shrinking. Globalization has created impending and colliding contingences of bordering realities. Cultural exchanges leave residual cultural and intellectual whirlpools where individuals and their communities negotiate the meaning of their identity in a tenuous relationship with their surroundings. It is a dynamic that is always oscillating, fluctuating, and negotiating identity. In the US this dynamic has different expressions and produces disparate opinions. Since this project has started there have been several incidents that show hostility towards the other. In 2014 children immigrants from Central America brought the notion of the outsider to the forefront. Later, the 2016 presidential race exposed radical sentiments of animosity towards Muslims and immigrants in general. Especially with the conflict in the Middle East it appears that the US still does not understand how to wrestle with the question of the other.

---

[1] The term 'Hispanic/Latin@' is designed to be inclusive of all the people from Latin America who may be present in the US. There are debates as to which term is proper to describe this multicultural, multinational, and multiethnic bloc. The term 'Hispanic' is a Nixonian creation and did not originate from the people themselves. The term 'Latino' may be problematic because those born in the US do not claim the term 'Latino'. It is also problematic for gender inclusion. I am aware of these issues and from here on out I shall use the term 'Latina' or 'Latino'. I am also aware of the need for gender inclusion. Although 'Latino' can refer to both genders, I prefer 'Latin@' as a designation for both 'Latina' and 'Latino'.

I approach the question of the other with the specific dimension of undocumented immigration to the US in full view. Undocumented immigration in the US by people from Latin America creates interesting contingencies in the negotiation of identity. As part of the Latino community in the US, I explore this notion of identity created by the peculiar vantage point of undocumented immigration. I also reflect theologically on this identity and what it means for an immigrant from Latin America. The reader must also be aware that I explore this point-of-view from the experience of a Honduran. In terms of the Latino community, Hondurans are a tiny slice of the Latin American community present in the United States.

I share my own origin so that the reader may be aware that my perspective may differ from that of other Latin Americans or Latinos in the US. Nonetheless, I explore this issue of identity to gain theological resources that enable the church to understand and address the contradictions and conundrums produced by undocumented immigration.

I begin with the notion of *mestizaje*. *Mestizaje* literally means intermixture, or miscegenation. It was also used as a pejorative term to describe the racial and cultural intermixing between Europeans and Natives in Latin America. It is now the locus theologicus of the Latino community in the US. This allows us a starting point where I can theologically explain the existence of subaltern communities of immigrants in North America. I believe that it is through *mestizaje* that one can begin a respectful dialogue that does justice and uplifts the humanity of undocumented immigrants in the US.

Contextual Background

In many ways this topic has been emotionally gut-wrenching for me personally. I am Honduran. And although I have never been an undocumented immigrant, I have experienced life as an immigrant in many countries by walking a fine line along the borderline of legality/illegality. I am the son of Honduran missionaries sent by a US-based denomination to the Philippines. Many people I met there had no idea where Honduras was on a map and it created interesting conversations with Filipino people. Later, I lived in the US during my university years going to school in a rural community in the

Southeastern US. Many students had no idea where the Philippines or Honduras were located. My Filipino assimilation further complicated my standing – even with fellow Latino peers – because it created interesting dialogue and interaction with fellow Latin@ students. I was a part of them but not easily recognized.

After my college experience I lived in Australia as a short-term missionary where people thought I was an Anglo-Saxon American merely because of my accent. Also, many did not readily understand what it meant for me to be Latino. Many talked with me reservedly, not knowing how to relate to me. More recently I lived in New York amidst the metropolitan cosmopolitan jungle full of different pockets of ethnic and racial diversity where I felt most at home.

I describe my particular experience because the issue of identity and the negotiation of this identity vis-à-vis a majority culture are central concerns for many immigrants and coexisting cultural groups. Furthermore, I hope not only that this book may be an aid for Latinos but that it may also may contribute to the self-understanding of many displaced and dislodged persons and communities living cross-culturally across the globe.

My main concern is to provide an entry-point to discuss undocumented immigration theologically. I have pastored two churches in the US where I have dealt directly with undocumented immigrants. Over time and through conversation I discovered that some of the church members did not have the proper documentation to live in the US. Their predicament in the church immediately created theological questions about the nature of the church as the body of Christ and where in the body they belonged. For example, since they were Christian I was forced to wrestle creatively with my understanding of their predicament in light of the coming Kingdom and their true heavenly citizenship in relation to their non-citizenship in the US. Their status in many ways was an analogy of Christians, who are described as being in this world but not a part of this world.[2] They were in the US, but not part of this society. However, through the church, they were one with us in Christ and pneumatologically affirmed as they experienced regeneration, sanctification, and the baptism of the Spirit.

---

[2] A similar insight is shared by Daniel Castelo, 'Resident and Illegal Aliens', *Apuntes* 23.2 (2003), pp. 65-77.

Dealing with these Christians' particular existential situation was also difficult. In one setting I remember dealing with a member who was paid less than minimum wage for arduous labor and who rented out the bathtub of a one-bedroom apartment that he shared with twelve other migrant workers. In other situations, I dealt with people who lived through situations where they could not drive or find good jobs. They were going hungry yet they decided to remain here. They also lived in constant fear of deportation – so much so that when they were robbed at gunpoint they did not report the incident to the police. I once answered a pastoral call in which a group of men in my congregation were robbed by armed men after they came home on Friday with their pay in cash. They were too scared to call the police. I told them it was necessary to do so and they consented. The police did an investigation but never found the assailants.

From my own point of view, I could not imagine the sort of reality that they left in their home countries for them to prefer to go through this type of subsistence in the US. Neither could I imagine the situation of their home countries that no matter how difficult things became in the US they preferred to stay. Some of them also dealt with the issue of separation where one or both parents were deported; and, consequently, families were split up since their children were born in the US.

This is the *raison d'être* for writing this book. Instead of polarizing debate, I want to take a more organic approach to understand first of all *who* these people are; and secondly, the reasons *why* they make the journey across deserts and without water or supplies to reach the US. It is easy to dismiss these people as law-breakers and aliens or a subaltern reality. It is too easy to see them as hopeless others without the capability of ever being one of us. In contrast, I have gotten to know many of them as fellow Christians who receive me into their homes and offer me they kind of hospitality that they themselves may have never received.

Mestizaje

In order to understand the issue theologically and organically, we must study *mestizaje*. Most studies of undocumented immigration deal with the immediacy of the situation, give histories of immigration, and collapse into a difficult discussion on rights, ethics, citizenship, and non-citizenship.[3] These are necessary studies. However, I think that to understand this phenomenon better and to give a better understanding of the existential crisis and the identity crisis these individuals face we can approach the subject theologically through *mestizaje*. If it becomes our starting point, I am convinced that we arrive at a more organic and responsible consideration of these people from the ground up. It gives them dignity without collapsing the argument into a polarizing debate on ethics and rights. And lastly, *mestizaje* creates necessary space for a compassionate look at those who have carried the unfortunate label: illegal aliens. This nomenclature alone dehumanizes them and creates a sense that they are hopelessly other.

Other theologians begin with the need to correct false perceptions about these immigrants. Harold Recinos in his text *Good News from the Barrio*, for example, describes the situation of Latinos in the inner city. More often than not, they experience poverty far exceeding that of most cultural groups in the US.[4] Recinos challenges the reader to avoid a covert type of racism, where people do not attack each other, but hide behind the cloak of propriety in order to exclude others from participation in society. He believes racism is embedded deep into American culture, and argues that this nation still maintains a hierarchical division of humanity into superior and inferior races.[5]

Recinos' relevance to this study, however, is his discussion of the power of representation, or of naming someone or something, particularly the case in which a name is applied to a group of people. Recinos invokes Charles Taylor's words: 'non-recognition or misrecognition can inflict harm, can be a form of oppression, impris-

---

[3] See the following texts: Samuel T. Francis, *The Sanctuary Movement: Smuggling Revolution* (Monterey, VA: American Immigration Control Foundation, 1986); Ignatius Bau, *This Ground is Holy: Church Sanctuary and Central American Refugees* (NY: Paulist Press, 1985); Ken Ellingwood, *Hard Line: Life and Death on the U.S.-Mexico Border* (NY: Vintage Books, 2005); Jim Corbett, *Goatwalking* (NY: Viking Penguin, 1991); Matthew Sorens and Jenny Hwang, *Welcoming the Stranger* (Downers Grove, IL: InterVarsity Press, 2009); R. Daniel Carroll, *Christians at the Border* (Grand Rapids: Baker Academic Press, 2008).

[4] Harold J. Recinos, *Good News from the Barrio: Prophetic Witness for the Church* (Louisville: Westminster John Knox Press, 2006), p. 16.

[5] Recinos, *Good News from the Barrio*, p. 19.

oning someone in a false, distorted, and reduced sense of being'.[6] There is a power manifest in naming someone or something. The symbol, the thing signified, and the intended meaning have powerful effects upon the human psyche. In recognizing the different dimensions of a symbol or of a particular name, Recinos challenges the church to move beyond stereotypes and prejudices in order to understand the diversity of Hispanic people and cultures that are affected through negative stereotypes.

These stereotypes have affected Hispanics in many negative ways. Recinos challenges the church because he believes it should not remain silent in light of racism, overt or covert. For instance, he decries the manner in which the church has kept silent in light of hatred and right-wing groups that seem to target Latinos. Recinos also addresses the issue of immigration, stating that it was obvious the US was not worried about undocumented immigrants until 9/11.[7]

Since 9/11, the rhetoric that is currently employed to discuss immigration is one of exclusion that can easily fuel ethnic violence. Many Hispanics blamed the language used by the media as fueling the scapegoating, violence, and hate crimes against these people. Furthermore, in the US, some individuals go as far as wanting to repeal the 14th Amendment of the US Constitution, a clause that establishes citizenship by birth in the US. If such a thing would ever happen, citizenship would only be extended to 'American' bloodlines. Some Americans thus behave as if 'true' Americans are White, Anglo-Saxon, and Protestant.

In light of such extremes, authors agree on the importance of a discussion on semantics. First and foremost, there is an unfortunate nomenclature that has been placed upon these immigrants. The term, illegal alien, is unhelpful, prejudicial, and a misnomer. Likewise, terminology like anchor babies and wetback, used by popular media impedes reasonable dialogue. R. Daniel Carroll provides a more helpful balanced understanding of the terminology used in describing immigrants. Perhaps the most important factor in addressing the immigration dilemma is in the use of terminology.

---

[6] Charles Taylor, 'The Politics of Recognition', in Amy Gutman (ed.), *Multiculturalism* (Princeton: Princeton University Press, 1994), pp. 25-74 (p. 25).

[7] Taylor, 'The Politics of Recognition', p. 21.

How one refers to undocumented immigrants reveals underlying prejudices and presuppositions concerning the issue. Like Recinos, Carroll describes the problem of semantics. He states that he prefers the term *undocumented immigrant* over *illegal alien*:

> Illegal carries a pejorative connotation, suggesting a person is guilty of some act, has few scruples, and is prone to civil disobedience … The term alien can evoke the sense of someone unchangeably foreign and other, without hope of reconciliation or mediation. Illegal alien, therefore, is unhelpfully prejudicial. Undocumented immigrant is a more just label and better represents the present reality.[8]

Furthermore, the term 'illegal' has had precedents such as 'new,' 'less desirable', and 'undesirable immigrants'.[9] Another reason these terms, both *illegal alien* and *illegal immigrant*, should not be used is due to the unfortunate history of the origin of these terms. Both were never used in reference to immigrants until the Chinese Exclusion Act of 1882. It is a term that cannot escape racist connotations.

Consequently, this terminology reveals a need to humanize the discourse; otherwise, there can be no genuine discussion of the issue. Any constructive discussion cannot take place when an individual or a community is dehumanized. Carroll believes that the overwhelming majority of Hispanics are law-abiding individuals and disagrees sharply with the frame of meaning the term illegal imposes upon these immigrants. In addition, they are not unchangeable and hopelessly foreign, like the term alien suggests. This is where I focus the discussion on *hibridez*. *Hibridez* is a term that I have introduced to this theological discourse. I appropriate it with a dialogue with *mestizaje* with postcolonial hybridity. It may seem disconnected. However, it has been used in postcolonial discourse to describe racial and cultural intermixture and is therefore similar to *mestizaje*. The main reason I use *hibridez* is that it describes encounters, liminal

---

[8] R. Daniel Carroll, *Christians at the Border: Immigration, Church, and the Bible* (Grand Rapids: Baker Academic), p. 22.

[9] Frank D. Bean, Barry Edmonston, and Jeffrey S. Passel, 'Perceptions and Estimates of Undocumented Migration to the United States', in Frank D. Bean, Barry Edmonston, and Jeffrey S. Passel (eds.), *Undocumented Migration to the US: IRCA and the Experience of the 1980's* (Washington, DC: Urban Institute Press, 1990), p. 13.

spaces, and allows the subject to take agency and responsibility in formation of identity. I also use it to describe intra-Latino tensions as well as a way to build bridges from the Latino community to those communities that Latinos come into contact with. *Hibridez* reveals a dynamic where immigrants from all places adapt and change and produce interesting fusions of culture in their nation of destination. More will be described below. Carroll believes that preferable terms should reflect the manner of their stay. Undocumented immigrants are persons who 1) *enter without inspection* (EWI's), or 2) who are *visa overstayers*.[10] The latter means they are allowed in the country legally and for some reason or other their visa expires before they are able to renew it or leave.[11]

Another author, Nick Spencer, enriches this discussion about nomenclature in his text, *Asylum and Immigration*. He believes that there are several other terms that can be used in order to seek understanding of the issues at stake in this discussion. Spencer gives a helpful list describing a better nomenclature, including the following terms: political migrant, economic migrant, immigrant, undocumented immigrant, asylum seeker, family settler, alien, and refugee.[12] Spencer believes that the underlying issue should be the question of relationship, for each term that is employed reveals the nature of the relationship between the host culture and its guest, and vice-versa. He later states that it is most helpful to seek to describe a more precise nature of the relationship:

> the relevant questions focus in on relationships – between community and individual, between native and immigrant, between population and environment, and between nation and nation. The Bible is nothing if it is not interested in relationships.[13]

The exhortation, then, is to focus on interrelationships. This forms the basis for a possible dialogue informed by hospitality

---

[10] Bean, Edmonston, and Passel, 'Perceptions and Estimates of Undocumented Migration to the United States', p. 3.

[11] The current timetable for anyone processing a visa is about 10 months to 2 years.

[12] Nick Spencer, *Asylum and Immigration: A Christian Perspective on a Polarised Debate* (Cambridge: Paternoser Press, 2004), p. 6. Spencer, unfortunately uses the term, 'illegal alien'. He does not use the term undocumented immigrant.

[13] Spencer, *Asylum and Immigration*, p. 70.

when addressing the issue of immigration. Unfortunately, North-American immigration policy is far more pragmatic than this, and in times of war and recession there is a prejudiced herd mentality of scapegoating those on the margins of society. Prejudicial terms, such as illegal alien, shut down discussion before it can begin. Nevertheless, theology must seek to humanize these immigrants and discuss the issue within reason.

I think the term, *mestizaje*, developed by the Latino theological community in the US, begins to give us the necessary space to discuss undocumented immigration from Latin America. It lets the immigrants speak for themselves, reducing stereotypes, and gives them the ability to name themselves. It also establishes a focus on interrelationships because it carries an idea of an exchange. *Mestizaje* also opens the door to *teología en conjunto*, or theology together as a team. By being grounded in *lo cotidiano*, *mestizaje* provides space to discuss immigration within a theological framework.

In a critical look at *mestizaje* we must come to terms with several issues that many authors have raised for us. I describe how *mestizaje* ultimately reveals issues of *hibridez*, and the struggle between the self and the other; as such, it is a theological concept upon which we are to build if we are to address the situation of undocumented immigrants from Latin America. In the theological field, the starting point in describing Latinos is the theological concept of *mestizaje*. *Mestizaje* is the *locus theologicus* or understanding the Latino theology in the US. However, there are many reasons why it still needs to be discussed and nuanced in current scholarship particularly from the vantage point of undocumented immigration and complemented with *hibridez*.

I propose that by means of a dialogue with *hibridez* we may understand the contextual realities of undocumented immigrants in the US. In a dialogue with *mestizaje*, I wish to come to terms with undocumented immigration and propose a genesis of a theology of undocumented immigration. It is through a discussion with *hibridez* that we can further provide ways of talking about undocumented immigration that point to the reasons and causes for undocumented immigration in the first place. It also helps us nuance this condition and look at the work of the Spirit of God in the midst of these people. *Hibridez* also points to the *cosmovisiones* of the people who make the journey to the US. Such *cosmovisiones* point to their way of being in the world. *Cosmovisión* is a term similar to worldview, but it carries its own profound significance. Through such a dialogue I hope to point out a web of relationality that characterizes these people and the complexity of how continual interactions with mainstream North American culture continue to shape them. Ultimately, I point to a relationship with the Spirit of God that moves us towards a hospitality oriented after God's Kingdom.

In what follows, I highlight a tension between *identitad* (identity) and *otredad* (otherness), a constant back-and-forth process that shapes these people through *hibridez*. It is a process that is mirrored in the tension between the immanent God and the transcendent God in Pentecostal praxis. This discussion of *hibridez* is not intended to replace *mestizaje* but to be a constant adjective qualifying *mestizaje*. This inclusion will help gain a sense of the diversity within Latin American peoples and the condition of undocumented immigration as adjusting and becoming subjects in their world. I hope that we may work for justice for them and find them a home in theology.

Hibridez also helps us analyze the religious symbols of the people. I shall examine the way *la Virgen de Guadalupe* and Jesucristo function in light of this *hibridez*. I shall also look at the method that this writing is applied through Sor Juana Inés de la Cruz. Later I make a pneumatological turn to see the way that *evangélicos* could apply a developing *hibridez* in their theological models especially in light of the phenomenological occurrences and experiences of the Spirit. It leads to a practical theology concerned with the human response to the divine and to considerations in the tension between transcendence and the immanence of the Spirit and how this may work as a model for interpersonal relationships. I look specifically at Azusa Street, knowing that what happened there continues to occur in Latin America. I am highlighting this particular location because it is a place where we find similar processes to an undocumented expression of Christianity today. I am not trying to ignore Latin America or expressions of Christianity there. My concern is to highlight the immigrants in Azusa Street at the turn of the century and the potential pneumatological insights that the work of the Spirit among immigrants may give us.

I also aim to dispel stereotypes about Latinos in the US as being all those south of the US-Mexico border. Latin Americans are more complex than the terminology currently employed to describe them leads us to think. It is necessary that we take each nationality and people group into special consideration rather than to stereotype them. For this reason, I shall interview Hondurans who happen to be a minute slice of the Latino community in the US. By focusing on Hondurans we shall see that even this tiny slice of the Latino community in the US is greatly diverse.

According to the Pew Center, a new nationwide survey found that most Hispanics do not embrace the term Hispanic and even fewer prefer the term Latino.[14] In this same survey 69 percent believe that they have different cultures, and only 29 percent thought that they had a common culture.[15] Most (51 percent) preferred to name themselves by their country of origin, such as Mexican–American, or Colombian-American, or Honduran-American. For pragmatic reasons, and in order to start from a place of familiarity from the community and current political climate, I begin with the term Latino. Nonetheless, I want to make it clear that those people who have inherited these labels question them.

I am convinced that each nationality deserves its unique consideration and can give a unique contribution to US Latino Theology. Part of this diversity includes Amerindian and other communities within Honduras. I have chosen this country because it is my background. I am Honduran-American. My aim in describing Honduras is not to focus the discussion exclusively upon immigration from Honduras but also to explore undocumented immigration as a phenomenon shared by various cultural groups in the margins of the various nations around the world. In other words, *mestizaje* can be a term that strives to understand the unique experiences of the Latino community in the US, but I am convinced that through *hibridez* it should also move outward to dialogue with other realities and move

---

[14] Paul Taylor, Mark Hugo López, Jessica Hamar Martínez, and Gabriel Velasco, 'When Hispanics Don't Fit: Hispanics and Their Views of Identity', The Pew Hispanic Center, http://www.pewhispanic.org/2012/04/04/when-labels-dont-fit-hispanics-and-their-views-of-identity/ (accessed April 4, 2012). See also, 'A Conversation about Identity', The Pew Hispanic Center, http://www.pewhispanic.org/2012/05/30/a-conversation-about-identity-tell-us-your-story/ (accessed May 30, 2012).

[15] Taylor, López, Martínez, and Velasco, 'When Hispanics Don't Fit: Hispanics and Their Views of Identity' (accessed April 4, 2012).

away from itself towards others. This is the reason for the inclusion of *hibridez*. I hope that by looking at *hibridez* we may move towards discovery of the other and how this leads to a demonstration of God's hospitality towards the immigrant and towards the other through his Holy Spirit.

A final dimension of this book proposes a hypothesis of what pneumatology would look like in light of undocumented immigration and a dialogue between *mestizaje* and *hibridez*. I am Pentecostal and as such I am concerned because there is minimal Pentecostal scholarship concerning undocumented immigration. This is also a reason I have chosen to interview undocumented immigrants in order to use their life stories as a resource for theology. In doing so, I follow the example of Ada María Isasi Díaz who used interviews as a resource for theological reflection. I also have to deal with several negative stereotypes in the Latino community in the US portraying Pentecostals as anti-intellectuals.[16] I believe that the lack of material from Pentecostals does not imply a lack of desire or an ambivalence to address this issue on their part. On the contrary, I am convinced that the reason we do not have more in-depth studies from a Pentecostal perspective is merely a matter of a lack of resources or access to these resources to write about this issue. The Academy is a place of privilege to which very few Latino Pentecostals have access.

Many Pentecostal pastors in the US are first-generation immigrants (some undocumented) who cannot afford education. Furthermore, they are bivocational, meaning they work and pastor at the same time. They live in communities where everyone is expected to work. Many do so for minimum wage. This lack of resources may be perceived as a problem; however, it is a tremendous opportunity for these *Pentecostales* because they live and do ministry among the immigrant poor in urban ghettos and among the marginalized in the US. In other words, these Pentecostals are the poor. Conversely, many undocumented immigrants actively adhere to a Pentecostal faith.

---

[16] See: Ada María Isasi-Díaz, *En la Lucha* (Minneapolis: Fortress Press, 1993), pp. 89, 152-54; and Virgilio Elizondo, *The Future is Mestizo* (Boulder, CO: University Press of Colorado, 2000), p. 69.

Instructions to the Reader

I must also tell the reader that since most theological exploration of my topic has been done from a Roman Catholic perspective, I must dialogue with the predominant Roman Catholic theologies of *mestizaje* in order to establish a particular Pentecostal perspective in a way that is able to dialogue with the main tradition as a whole. Also, most immigrants come from a Roman Catholic background and this understanding informs Pentecostalism.[17] Nonetheless, I think a Pentecostal perspective may contribute to our understanding of undocumented immigration, *mestizaje*, and *hibridez*.

I am also aware that my particular Pentecostal perspective is not commonly represented in the Academy and the amount of material for this type of work is extremely limited. There is a general lack of resources from a Pentecostal perspective addressing undocumented immigration. In many ways I am doing a Pentecostal rereading of Roman Catholic *mestizaje*. However, I also mimic what *Pentecostales* already do: they elaborate on their Roman Catholic roots with a new dimension of the work of the Holy Spirit.[18] I do this to advocate for a theology of immigration that is humane, just, and grounded theologically. I realize that I am treading new ground. In doing so, I borrow and appropriate theological terms and concepts that other theologians have used in different ways. However, I hope to interact, validate, and synthesize a variety of authors and put together a theology from a Pentecostal perspective.

The theologians I discuss wrote during specific times, for specific motives, and specific contexts. Their comments, ideas, and usage of terminology may seem out of context in regard to what I am trying to do in this book, but I will do my best to adapt them to my context as a Pentecostal concerned with undocumented immigration while respecting their particular perspectives.

I also hope the reader maintains an open mind when discussing undocumented immigrants to the US. It is an emotionally-charged and polarizing topic for many people. However, I hope we can take a more humanizing look at one of the most extreme ways of living

---

[17] See Miguel Álvarez's forthcoming discussion on the way Roman Catholicism informs Pentecostalism in integral mission in *Beyond Borders: New Contexts of Mission in Latin America* (Cleveland, TN: CPT Press, 2017 forthcoming).

[18] Álvarez, *Beyond Borders*, forthcoming.

in the US. I also hope the reader can have a mind that is open to discussing undocumented immigration from an emerging Pentecostal perspective.

My theological proposal centers on the perspective of pneumatic peoples, and more specifically *los Pentecostales*, who make the journey across the Sonoran Desert in route to the US. Jacqueline Hagan states that they may represent as much as 25% of all those who cross the desert.[19] *Pentecostales* have a particular *manera de ser* (way of being in the world).[20] I not only seek to address a way of being Latino in the world, but also a way of being Pentecostal. The reality of pneumatic people making their way *al Norte* leads to overlapping identities as being Latinos and as being *Pentecostales*.

Statement of Human Research

Because of the nature of this material whenever I interview a person they have asked me to maintain their anonymity for their protection. To honor this request, I have changed their names wherever it is appropriate, avoided questions concerning their immigrant status, and have focused my comments exclusively on those who have voluntarily given that information to me. While I have interviewed several individuals and families, I only include those who freely indicated their undocumented status without prying or asking them directly about it.

---

[19] Jacqueline Hagan, 'Faith for the Journey', in Daniel G. Groody and Gioacchino Campese (eds.), *A Promised Land, A Perilous Journey* (Notre Dame: University of Notre Dame Press, 2008), pp. 3-19 (p. 16). This study puts the number of Protestant immigrants at 25% of a sample group. None of them claimed to be mainline Protestant. She also includes Mormons and Jehovah's Witnesses as part of the Protestant groups. In order to avoid further stereotypes, I wish to use the term *evangélic@* interchangeably with *pentecostales*, for in Latin America *evangélic@s* are understood to be Pentecostal. In English the term evangelical refers almost exclusively to the Christian right. Nonetheless, because of the connotations that it has in English, I wish to present undocumented immigrants and Pentecostality as an alternate part of this evangelical community. An evangelical perspective may also be diverse in that it may include the marginalized, poor, undocumented immigrant. These may also lean left.

[20] James K.A. Smith, *Thinking in Tongues: Pentecostal Contributions to Christian Philosophy* (Grand Rapids: Eerdmans, 2010), pp. 31-32.

2

MESTIZAJE: ORIGINS AND CONSTRUCTIVE WORK

Introduction

In this chapter I examine the origins and development of *mestizaje* as the *locus theologicus* of Latin@ theology.[1] In order to establish a niche from which to understand undocumented immigration it is important to understand *mestizaje*. *Mestizaje* is central to this study because it serves as a dynamic philosophical identity descriptor and not just an ethnic and racial descriptor for theology in the US Latino community, and as such it reveals a way of being, thinking, and acting in the world as Latino. In other words, it reveals the community's *cosmovisión*. Thus to understand the plight of undocumented immigrants, I believe we must first understand *mestizaje*. It will allow us to understand who these immigrants are, and why they make the journey to *al norte*.

An Overview of *Mestizaje*

Néstor Medina wrote a text describing the development of *mestizajes*.[2] Medina is a theologian concerned with *mestizaje* and cultural exchanges. In his text, *mestizaje*, he describes three different streams

---

[1] From this point forward, I use the form Latino. The reason for this is to avoid confusion in the several different terms used in the community.

[2] *Mestizajes* is in plural form here and is the preferred term by Néstor Medina. The underline is mine in order to acknowledge and emphasize the plurality that term defines.

of thought within this tradition. He calls the first Roman Catholic theology, the second Chicano theology, and the final secular readings of *mestizaje*. A thorough exploration of these three streams of thought and of Néstor Medina goes outside the scope of my discussion. Here my focus is on the origin and development of *mestizaje* as the *locus theologicus* of US Latino theology. Therefore, I examine the contextual and historical factors that led to this term's use in theology.

US Latino theologians such as Virgilio Elizondo and Ada María Isasi Díaz embraced *mestizaje* as a term to make sense of their context and their respective Mexican and Cuban heritages in the US. They used *mestizaje* to reclaim their history despite sociocultural marginalization in the US.[3] Furthermore, they sought to affirm their identity through *mestizaje*, particularly when the rest of the academy was fixated exclusively on a White vs. Black discourse. This term is also important because the US Latino population has always resisted assimilationist ideals in the US, maintaining strong ties to their culture, foods, and even choices of entertainment. This contrasts sharply with European immigrants that have blended in with each other. For Elizondo and Isasi-Díaz, *Mestizaje* explained their differences and identity, and allowed Latinos to reclaim their history. It also became the locus for theological reflection because it affirmed their particular culture and their particular religious practices in the US. Even within Roman Catholicism, *mestizaje* affirmed their particular popular religion. The practices and customs of the people were not merely aberrations of Christianity.

Mestizaje also reveals powerful currents of biological and cultural intermixture.[4] For instance, many Latinos present in the US are an intermixture of White, Black, Amerindian, and other groups. *Mestizaje* thus affirms their uniqueness and resists assimilationist tendencies. It also demonstrates the complexity of a Latino identity when it comes to ethnic and racial markers. This complexity formed a gestalt to fashion a theology from the particular experiences from Latin America. It also drew attention and thought because of paral-

---

[3] Néstor Medina, *Mestizaje: Mapping race, culture and faith in Latina/o Catholicism* (Maryknoll, NY: Orbis Books, 2009), p. xi.

[4] Medina, *Mestizaje*, p. x.

lel cultural intermixtures between the Spanish dominated colonial era in Latin America and the experiences of Latinos in the US.

Elizondo and Isasi-Díaz affirmed their identity as unique. This, in turn, provoked a systematic rereading of the biblical text and of the various theological traditions these scholars inherited from North American and European theology.[5] Consequently, US Latino theologians reconfigured these theological tasks, methods, and sources that led to a rethinking of these traditions.[6] Néstor Medina further points out that theology, doctrine, and biblical interpretation was open to re-inspection and rereading with regard to questions of class, gender, culture, and race.[7] In the 1960s, several Roman Catholic scholars began reflecting on their Latino identity.[8] Such reflections generated ACHTUS, or the Academy of Catholic Hispanic Theologians, and the establishment of the *Journal of Hispanic/Latino Theology*.

These reflections continue as Latinos negotiate their identity vis-à-vis US culture. Part of the first hurdle that many people had to face was the acknowledgment (or lack thereof) that Latinos have always been present in the US. Medina gives several examples of what was an ignored portion of the US population.[9]

Medina's Hispanic/Latin@ Presence in the US

First, Mexicans have lived in the US before it gained independence from Britain. Florida, Texas, and the Southwest were at one point a part of the Spanish Empire. Furthermore, the aftermath of the Manifest Destiny and the Mexican–American War immediately placed thousands of Mexicans on the US side of the border. Some included Amerindian groups, like the Tarahumara, who have since then roamed back and forth through the US-Mexico border.[10]

Other historic causalities placed even more Latino peoples in the US. One such event is the Spanish American War of 1898. This event created a steady flow of Puerto Ricans and Cubans into the US *en masse*. In 1917 Puerto Ricans were granted full US citizenship.

---

[5] Medina, *Mestizaje*, p. xi.

[6] Medina, *Mestizaje*, p. x.

[7] Medina, *Mestizaje*, p. x.

[8] Medina, *Mestizaje*, p. xii.

[9] Medina, *Mestizaje*, p. xii.

[10] Christopher McDougall, *Born to Run: A Hidden Tribe, Superathletes, and the Greatest Race the World Has Never Seen* (New York: Knopf Doubleday, 2009), p. 17.

To this day Puerto Rico continues in tension with the US in a unique relationship as a dependent territory with unique independent rights. Cubans who gained prominence in the US after the Cuban Revolution were given special provisions after the Communist victory on the island. The Cuban immigrants to the US faced unique experiences of identity and immigration.

Mexicans who became US citizens after the Mexican–American War continued to experience unique tensions in their stay in the US. Many more continued to arrive in the US after bitter conflict in their homelands. Even more were lured by work opportunities in the US. One example was the Bracero program that opened the doors to manual labor such as farm work for immigrants in the 1960's. Many of these laborers ended up staying in the US.

The influx of these immigrants raised issues of identity because they did not fit neatly in Black-White categories. In terms of religion and the church, the Catholic Church in the US was dominated by priests of European descent who viewed the popular religion of Puerto Ricans, Cubans, and Mexicans with condescension and as inferior expressions of piety. Furthermore, tensions became greater as in the 1970s there was also a boom of Puerto Rican immigrants in New York City.[11] During the same decade, the US government appropriated the term Hispanic to a people they did not understand, labeling a diverse people with an overarching descriptor that many of them seemed to reject.

Medina's Perspective on Theological Appropriation of *Mestizaje*

In the Academy, Liberation Theology figured prominently in North and Latin American reflections. It is within this context that Virgilio Elizondo began to propose the usage of the term *mestizaje* as a theological concept. He picked up several liberationist undercurrents from Medellín in 1968.[12] Elizondo found himself particularly critical of theological reflections in the Academy that were locked in a fervent Black-White discourse. Elizondo became aware that there was no niche or no particular category from which to do theology

---

[11] Medina, *Mestizaje*, p. xiii.
[12] Medina, *Mestizaje*, p. xiv.

for and from his people who had a particular experience of marginalization.[13]

Through his usage of *mestizaje*, Elizondo found a way to debunk racial stereotypes, and to theologize from the experience of marginalization. This usage also became a way of affirming the people's faith by insisting on their own particular understanding of Roman Catholicism.[14] Elizondo's reflections demonstrated that Mexican–Americans were not superstitious nor did they have childish customs. Rather, they had a particular contribution to make for theology and a particular way to do theology.

Other theologians followed Elizondo and appropriated *mestizaje* in their reflection, expanding on Elizondo's understanding. A prime example was Ada María Isasi-Díaz, a Roman Catholic scholar. She also voiced a concern for the women of the church in their context of oppression. She informed *mestizaje* through *lo cotidiano* and *la lucha por supervivencia* and used her particular understanding from the Cuban American experience to introduce the notions of *mujerista theology* and *mulatez* in theology.

Néstor Medina describes an ensuing boom in *mestizo* theology in the late 1980s and in the early 1990s.[15] Several theologians used and appropriated the theological term of *mestizaje*. Medina gives several examples like Robert Goizueta, who described a distinct theological method using *mestizaje*.[16] Also, María Pilar Aquino also adopted *mestizaje* in order to do reflections for her people.[17] Eldin Villafañe described *mestizaje* as the central identity marker though he described it as three distinct streams interacting with one another.[18] Such efforts led to later formulations such as De La Torre's volume *Introduction to Latina/o Theology* that uses *mestizaje* as the main theme.[19]

---

[13] Medina, *Mestizaje*, p. xv.

[14] Hector Elizondo, *Galilean Journey: The Mexican–American Promise* (Maryknoll, NY: Orbis Books, 2000), p. 9.

[15] Medina, *Mestizaje*, p. xvii.

[16] Roberto Goizueta, *Caminemos con Jesús: Towards a Hispanic/Latino Theology of Accompaniment* (Maryknoll, NY: Orbis Books, 1995); *and* Medina, *Mestizaje*, p. xvii.

[17] Maria Pilar Aquino, *Our Cry for Life: Feminist Theology from Latin America* (Maryknoll, NY: Orbis Books, 1993), and Medina, *Mestizaje*, xvii.

[18] Eldin Villafañe, *The Liberating Spirit: Toward an Hispanic American Social Ethic* (Grand Rapids: Eerdmans, 1993), pp. 194-95.

[19] Miguel A. De La Torre and Aponte, *Handbook of Latina/o Theologies* (Duluth: Chalice Press, 2006); and Medina, *Mestizaje*, p. xviii.

However, it was in this same decade that more prominent critiques adopted the term. Néstor Medina states that US Latino theologians developed *mestizaje* and broadened its meaning and applicability.[20] However, in asserting distinctiveness from the sociocultural and theological context of Latin America, Medina states that they failed to pay attention to the Latin American context and hegemonic expressions of *mestizaje*.[21] They uncritically adopted *mestizaje* without noting the problems it created in the Latin American context.[22] The crux of the matter was that these theologians sought parallels between the original experience of discrimination of the *mestizo* children by their indigenous and Spanish ancestors to their new experience of marginalization in the US.[23] However, Medina notes how these formulations faced strong critiques from Latin America, particularly from the lens of the poor and non-mestizos in Latin America.[24] This is important to note and we shall give necessary space to these critiques later in this book. However, at the moment we shall focus on the origins of *mestizaje* and how Roman Catholic theologians articulated a contextualized theology from *mestizaje*. I examine first Virgilio Elizondo and secondly Ada María Isasi-Díaz.

Virgilio Elizondo and *Mestizaje*

Some call Virgilio Elizondo the father of US Latino religious thought.[25] He currently teaches at Notre Dame University and explores applications of *mestizaje* to interpret the past and to build the future. Elizondo's work is important for this discussion because he was one of the first theologians that addressed the need for understanding the Latino presence in the US. Elizondo's contribution is that he sought to understand the Mexican–American presence in a society that did not seem to understand them (and still doesn't). He

---

[20] Medina, *Mestizaje*, p. xviii.

[21] Medina, *Mestizaje*, p. xviii.

[22] Medina, *Mestizaje*, p. xviii.

[23] Medina, *Mestizaje*, p. xviii, also see Elizondo, *Galilean Journey*, p. 10.

[24] Medina, *Mestizaje*, p. xviii.

[25] Oscar García-Johnson, *The Mestizo/a Community of the Spirit: A Postmodern Latino/a Ecclesiology* (Eugene: Pickwick Publications, 2009), p. 31. See also the 'Virgilio Elizondo' by the Department of Theology, University of Notre Dame, http://theology.nd.edu/people/all/elizondo-virgilio/ (accessed December 11, 2011).

wrote about the unique characteristics, understandings, and thoughts of their people. Contrary to what some perceived, Mexican–Americans did not practice an aberration of Roman Catholicism nor did they have an inferior perspective of Christianity. Elizondo, however, sought to understand the Mexican–American community on its own terms.

Elizondo's contribution is invaluable because he explores his people's identity and why they are present in the US. He affirms his people when he asserts that *mestizaje* is a way of being in the world that emerges out of a shared colonial past through forced ethnic and racial mixing. Furthermore, *mestizaje* holds together their world, popular religion, and theological beliefs. Elizondo uses *mestizaje* to recognize the social location of the Mexican–American people and to demonstrate a respect for their cultural traditions. As an identity marker, *mestizaje* acts as a hermeneutical and analytical tool for theology. It incorporates their *cosmovisión* and as such it becomes the *locus theologicus* of theology.

Elizondo admits that Gustavo Gutiérrez's *Teología de Liberación* motivated him: 'to see the suffering of the poor, to hear their cries, and to enter into their quest for liberation'[26] within the North-American context. He dedicated his work to empower Mexican–Americans in the US so that even in the midst of poverty they might 'dare to dream and begin something new'.[27] Furthermore, Elizondo also worked 'to make the structures of society work in favor of and to create a new knowledge about ourselves, our social situation, and religious beliefs'.[28] For Elizondo, *mestizaje* informs theology with the socio-cultural situation of Mexican–Americans present in the US.

Commonality/Universality and Specificity

One of the first dimensions I note of his usage is a Latino universality or commonality through the usage of *mestizaje*. For example, though he focuses exclusively on Mexican–Americans many theologians cite Elizondo's theology as applicable to the other Latino

---

[26] Virgilio Elizondo, 'Mestizaje as a Locus of Theological Reflection', in Arturo Bañuelas (ed.), *Mestizo Christianity: Christianity from a Latino Perspective* (Maryknoll, NY: Orbis, 1995), p. 7.

[27] Elizondo, 'Mestizaje as a Locus of Theological Reflection', p. 9.

[28] Elizondo, 'Mestizaje as a Locus of Theological Reflection', p. 9.

peoples. Thus, there are two movements in *mestizaje* by Elizondo. One is very specific that describes Mexican–Americans. A second dimension is that it may also relate to the collective identity of other Latinos in the US. Therefore, there is a commonality in *mestizaje* that brings in diverse and alternate Latin American communities. This is a dimension that has recently faced much critique.

The colonial dimension implicit in *mestizaje* buttresses the commonality that directly and indirectly influenced the formation of *mestizos*. Because these different groups have many things in common with the experience of colonization one may find common threads concerning these experiences in *mestizaje* and as pertaining to their genesis and formation.

It is also a term that is shared by many groups because Elizondo uses it to refer to ongoing cultural changes these people face when they arrive in the US. As these people enter the US, they face the internalization of *mestizaje* and come to terms with the North American experience. This dynamism is parallel to that experienced with colonial Latin America and leads to a second *mestizaje*, that with US mainstream society and culture.

Expanding the Function of *Mestizaje*

Elizondo's work describes how the term *mestizo* was originally a pejorative racial term because it was used to demarcate social and power structures in a colonial society that was defined along racial lines. In these societies, European-born whites were considered the top of the socio-cultural and colonial system.[29] These were followed in the hierarchical scheme by *criollos*, or European whites born in the Americas. These had many privileges because of their European ancestry, but were considered inferior because of their lack of direct contact with Europe. Next in this colonial scheme came *indios*. Their race as well as their lack of contact with Europe made them inferior. In many cases, they were enslaved or forced to work for the Spaniards.

---

[29] Michelle A. González, 'Who Is Americana/o', in Catherine Keller, Michael Nausner, and Mayra Rivera (eds.), *Postcolonial Theologies: Divinity and Empire* (St. Louis: Chalice Press, 2004), pp. 58-78. See her discussion on pp. 64-65. Many of the Spaniards had already experienced a mixture with the invasion from the Moors.

This racial delineation was a consequence of the Spanish feudal system in which one had to prove allegiance to the Spanish crown. Often times this was done through one's genealogy.[30] *Mestizaje* became a way to demonstrate allegiance to the crown and a way to demonstrate the adaptation into Spanish society. The result of the imperial systems of the Spanish and Portuguese were peoples from Europe, Africa, and Asia meeting with Amerindians in the Americas. This led to a complex social system where people looked for favor with the ruling entities. It led to a formation of a system of ethnic identity demarcating power, but it did not remain this simple.[31]

Michelle González describes how in the conquest of colonial territories and due to the lack of Spanish women in Latin America, Spanish men took native women as wives and hetaerae.[32] This dimension of colonial life was a cruel reality because of the violence and exploitation these women experienced at the hands of the Spaniards. González states that one cannot sanitize the history of this mixture.[33] A new people emerged in the American continent. These were called *mestizos,* and in the grand scheme of society they were considered above *indios,* but inferior to European-born Spaniards and *criollos.* Over time, however, the peoples of Latin America experienced a gradual and continual mixture so that these people cohabited and carried out their way-of-life as community in spite of colonial racial taboos. The result was a society that incorporated dimensions of Amerindian, African, and European cultures, with the dominant motif being that of the Iberian influence.[34]

Elizondo argues that for the people of Latin American descent *mestizaje* is important because it evokes this history of Latin America as a factor that must be considered when describing Latinos. Authors, such as John Frederick Schwaller, describe how the tension built up from a history of power struggles in Latin America erupted

---

[30] John Frederick Schwaller, *The History of the Catholic Church in Latin America: From Conquest to Revolution and Beyond* (New York: New York University Press, 2011), pp. 1-5.

[31] Schwaller, *The History of the Catholic Church in Latin America,* p. 5.

[32] González, 'Who Is Americana/o', p. 66.

[33] González, 'Who Is Americana/o', p. 66.

[34] See also Villafañe, *The Liberating Spirit,* pp. 3-11.

in violence, civil war, and revolution in the 20th century.[35] Thus, *mestizaje* evokes the history of Latin America to be considered as a factor in their ethos and formation even in the 21st century. I propose it is also a term that must be considered relating to existential and phenomenological push factors that create undocumented migration.

Mestizaje: Beyond Racial Categories

First, *Mestizaje* and its proper understanding push beyond racial stereotypes and call for a reevaluation of our understanding of Latinos. Racially, one may appear black or white but identify with his or her Latino ethnicity. This produces tensions between race and ethnicity that seem ignored by US politics, as well as tensions that contrast sharply to an exclusive Black-White discourse.

Secondly, *mestizaje* captures notions and ideas of violence in Latin America. The history of violence is one that cannot be measured, especially when dealing with the consequences on generations: chronic poverty, violence, along with malady of impunity for this violence in Latin America. These are dimensions that are essential reasons why these people leave their home countries to seek a better way of life somewhere else. Martin Stabb states that the early history of a group of people exerts much influence on their future development.[36] So it is with *mestizaje's* history.

The US Experience

Elizondo describes the influence of history upon Mexican–Americans in relation to their experience in the US. For example, the US government decided that Mexicans were to be considered white after the Mexican–American War, although many of them did not identify with Anglo culture in the US. *Mestizaje* for Elizondo, then, is a term he employs to name himself and his community, thus liberating himself and his people from racial stereotypes that have been imposed on the Mexican–American people from the outside. It is a term that also allows him to appreciate his dark-skinned ancestry. He describes that the dark-skinned Amerindian ancestry of his people influenced and continues to influence their *cosmovisión*;

---

[35] Schwaller, *The History of the Catholic Church in Latin America*, p. 4.

[36] Martin Stabb, *In Quest of Identity* (Chapel Hill: The University of North Carolina Press, 1967), p. 190.

the Mexican–American community is an amalgamation of this and Iberian heritages.

For Elizondo, this term provides the necessary space for the dominant culture in the US to understand a Mexican–American *cosmovisión y realidad* to such a degree that *mestizaje* is not merely a racial descriptor but a way of being in the world. It includes the practices of Mexican–Americans, as well as their way of thinking. This *cosmovisión* is not a static set of propositional truths but a socially imaginative dynamic. Because it incorporates their *cosmovisión*, it also becomes the *locus theologicus* for the church. Thus for Elizondo, *mestizaje* is more than a mere descriptor for the race or ethnicity of the Mexican–American people. Other theologians agree and apply his thought as a descriptor for the entire Latino spectrum in the US. *Mestizaje* serves as a departure point for theological reflection.[37]

A Second Mestizaje

Furthermore, Elizondo's incorporation of *mestizaje* is also conscious of another dimension of angst present in Latino life in the US. They experience a second *mestizaje* – that with US mainstream culture. This *mestizaje* is complex because it incorporates the idea of the internalization of *mestizaje* and a constant struggle with their identity in the US. It describes the constant struggle Latinos have within their new surroundings. It also describes the struggle new immigrants have in their adopted homeland.

Elizondo uses the example of the Annexation of Northern Mexico by the US to understand the second *mestizaje* as a turbulent experience and as one that has not always been easy for any people entering the US. For example, after the Mexican–American War (1846-1848), thousands of Mexicans found themselves on the US side of the new border; and, therefore, they became citizens of the US by force. Elizondo describes how these peoples experienced exclusion in their own lands after this war, and some were stripped of their ancestral lands. Furthermore, perhaps due to social taboos and other racial, cultural, and ethnic taboos and barriers these people did not readily mix with their counterparts in this new nation.

Such a condition produced what Elizondo describes as an internalization of *mestizaje* with negative connotations that continues to

---

[37] See, for example, Goizueta, *Caminemos con Jesús*.

mark and shape Mexican–Americans in the US. For Mexican immigrants, Mexican–Americans, and *Chicanos*, their ethos is marked by a constant angst. They are a people twice colonized, first by the European Spaniards and secondly by the US. The latter colonization began in the 1830s and was highlighted by the Mexican–American War.

Elizondo highlights this internalization of *mestizaje* as a way-of-being characterized by 'a deeper violence of disruption and attempts to destroy the conquered's inner worldvision, which gives cohesion and meaning to existence'.[38] Thus, for Elizondo, *mestizaje* is not just a racial or cultural identifier but also an important philosophical descriptor of the clash of worldviews and the resulting fallout marked by an existence etched out in the wake of this clash. This is also a dimension that applies to a broader Latino body and appeals to the universality of a disruptive cultural experience.

Contributions from Elizondo

Elizondo's contribution is immensely important; he retrieves the term *mestizo* historically and reclaims it theologically thereby affirming the Mexican–American *cosmovisión*. In other words, this term does not have to remain in a negative, racist light. Elizondo explains that far from being exclusively a pejorative term, *mestizaje* is an important ethnic, cultural, ideological, and theological term. He calls it 'the border reality that characterizes the Latino experience of being people "in between"'.[39] In other words, it is a term that explains the crisis and process of being in between two cultures and experiencing ruptures and mixtures. Later, this leads to the usage of this term in a broader sense including the collective Latin American community in the US.

Elizondo is hopeful in his exploration because he invites the reader to explore new and future *metizajes*. It is a term that may have important contributions for the near future as different racial groups in the US are increasingly mixing. The future of the US is increasingly a mixed reality.[40] *Mestizaje* though originating in the La-

---

[38] Elizondo, 'Mestizaje as a Locus for Theological Reflection', p. 10.

[39] Elizondo, *Galileean Journey*, p. 18.

[40] Susan Saulny, 'Black? White? Asian? More Young Americans Choose All of the Above', *The New York Times* (January 30, 2011), http://www.nytimes.com/2011/01/30/us/30mixed.html?ref=us (accessed January 30, 2011).

tino community should not remain locked in an inescapable ghetto. In this increasingly globalized age, the future is open for more *mestizajes* to occur. Elizondo shifts his usage to a more universal sense. In the Spanish, *mestizaje* simply means a mixture of races, or culture. However, more recent Latin American critiques question the way this term is employed. I shall give attention to these below.

In studying Elizondo, a pattern that many Latino theologians follow emerges. He describes the people's struggles for survival. He also depicts these people as always being on the underside of history, resisting domination and oppressive civilizations. Furthermore, he makes sense of a *mestizo* identity as related to the future as it relates to those on the fringes of the dominant culture. The focus of his study is on understanding his people's identity and how to live in the daily reality of mixture and interrelatedness. For Elizondo, one can make sense of this process and move to a new *mestizaje*, preserving Latino traditions and roots. He provides a way to break free from stereotypes by providing a name for his community.

Mestizaje also points to the history of Latin America. It informs us as to who these people are, and why they make their journey *al Norte*. We must consider the reason they choose to leave their home countries and enter the US. They do not come here simply because the US is rich. There is something more primal and evil at stake: when people are forced to make a decision whether to immigrate or go hungry it is the most sensible choice to immigrate. Thus, *mestizaje* begins to provide a humanized look at immigrants and those who do not easily fit in US categories.

Problems with Elizondo's Conceptualization of *Mestizaje*

Elizondo's conceptualization is important for us to understand Latinos in the US. However, there are problems that we must look over and recognize so that we can also apply this beyond the Mexican–American community. There is a tension among divergent experiences from Latin America that makes *mestizaje* a very slippery term because every nation in Latin America has its own history and all have experienced types of *mestizajes* in different ways. *Mestizaje* is a term that can be used in a general sense as mixture, or in much more specific sense as a mixed Amerindian and white person.

In this case, Elizondo focuses it down specifically and narrows it down to the Mexican–American experience. This may become complicated because there is a rising awareness of other Latinos in the US or other peoples from Latin America, as more complex than originally thought. More recent scholarship notes the exclusion of *mulatez*, or the Afro-Latino peoples, when it comes to *mestizaje*.[41] Such a description could also be interpreted as marginalizing and excluding indigenous groups from Latin America. Furthermore, there is a great diversity of Amerindian people that also make their way *al norte*, some of whom first learn Spanish upon entering the US. Mexico alone has over 60 recognized languages other than Spanish or English. Indigenous people in Mexico also have the right to use their own language in official government proceedings.

A narrow application of *mestizaje* could be interpreted as not acknowledging the humanity of people who do not happen to have any sort of mixture with European whiteness.[42] It could also be interpreted that Elizondo's version of *mestizaje* excludes other Latin American peoples present in the US, as well as descendants Arab, Palestinian, Chinese, and African immigrants who happen to be in Latin America.

Also, there are Mexican–Americans that are of European-only descent that have not been on the underside of history. Some have enjoyed privileges, such as wealth and entitlement, that have allowed them to escape the underside of their realities. This reveals an ongoing tension within the Latino community in the US in which there are commonalities, but at the same time there are differences. It is a tension between particularities and the whole.

Another major omission on the part of Elizondo is the lack of any specific mention of undocumented immigration and the way this ties in historically to the Mexican–American community and the way in which this reality can be addressed theologically. Elizondo writes of the Mexican–American community and of migrant workers, but I think there should be more scholarship in the area of undocumented immigration particularly because of the many undocumented workers from Mexico (as well as those from many other countries) in the US. Nonetheless, I think Elizondo's work on *mestizaje* provides a necessary historical grounding that serves as a

---

[41] Medina, *Mestizaje*, p. 106.

[42] Miguel A. De La Torre, 'Rethinking Mulatez', in Miguel A. De La Torre and Gastón Espinosa (eds.), *Rethinking Latino(a) Religion and Identity* (Cleveland: Pilgrim Press, 2006), pp. 158-75 (p. 159).

starting point to describe and understand the plight of undocumented immigrants in the US.

Conclusions on Elizondo

A study of Elizondo reveals that there are tensions within *mestizaje*. It also reveals tensions from *mestizaje* to other communities from Latin America and the Caribbean present in the US. *Mestizaje* is useful in a general sense to describe the reality of being bilingual, multiracial, and multicultural. It also points us to borders or borderlands because it is there that new *mestizajes* in the general sense of mixtures are produced. *Mestizaje* must be informed with a back-and-forth movement, or dialectic tension between the cultures and/or races and *encuentros* (encounters) and *encontronazos* (collisions) with these mixtures. Furthermore, Elizondo's understanding of *mestizaje* must always be open to and be enriched by others from Latin America and beyond. This is an essential element in understanding *mestizaje*, as one has to deal with ethnic, racial, and national differences *within* and *with those outside* of Latino peoples.

There are very useful and positive elements in Elizondo's theology. *Mestizaje* calls theology to be grounded on and engaged in the daily struggles of Latin@s for survival. In its methodology the historical subjects are *los de abajo* (the underdogs, or literally, the ones from below). He gives examples of nontraditional places from which theology arises such as the unskilled worker, the single mother on welfare, the migrant, the poet, the prison inmate, the political refugee, the low-paid housekeeper, the *abuelita*, and the abandoned children.[43] These become essential subjects in formulating theology.

From Elizondo we gain a sense that *mestizo* theology is a reflection of the faith dimension in the Latino struggle for life. It is grounded in these daily life-struggles and hopes of Latinos trying to survive a dominant culture. For Elizondo, Latino theology's primary source of reference is the activity of God who is forming a humanity that is sensitive to the intricate brush-strokes involved in the creation of a *mestizo* people and their racial, cultural, and ethnic identities. Nonetheless, it becomes necessary to include more of the experiences from Latin America.

---

[43] Elizondo, *Galilean Journey*, p. 55.

3

EXPANDING *MESTIZAJE*

Introduction

I now examine another author who expands *mestizaje* and its usage, Ada María Isasi-Díaz. Her writings serve as an example to follow as we seek to understand undocumented immigration. Isasi-Díaz is an important author for the Latino community in the US. One of her main contributions was that she expanded on *mestizaje* theologically from a Cuban-American perspective. She was born in La Habana, Cuba and experienced the Cuban Revolution. She immigrated to the US along with her family as a child. One of her main contributions is the perspective of the Cuban-American experience in the US.

Ada María Isasi Díaz was best known for describing the experience of *mujeres Latinas* in the US. She was the founder and co-director of the Hispanic Institute of Theology at Drew University. Her best-known text was *Mujerista Theology*, published in 1996. She passed away in early 2012, leaving behind a tremendous legacy to those who follow in her footsteps.

Isasi-Díaz and *Mestizaje*'s Tension between Particularity and Generality

I focus on Isasi-Díaz because of the specific contributions she makes for theology. Isasi-Díaz further nuances Elizondo's theology of *mestizaje* by adopting and developing a mutuality and solidarity that takes into consideration a more expansive understanding of *mestizaje* derived from the diverse racial and ethnic mixes in the US Latino community. She introduces several streams of thought contributing to and expanding *mestizaje* usefully: through the experience of *mulatez*, the daily struggle for life *lo coditiano*, and women in *mujerista theology*.

She sees subtexts and intermixtures inherent in a discussion on *mestizaje* and points the way to a connection to a transcultural *hibridez* that allows for the inclusion of different elements of the Latino community. For Isasi-Díaz *mulatez* and *mujerista* theology are ideas that resist cultural assimilation and acculturation. She reveals a *cosmovisión* based on survival (*supervivencia*). In her thought there are alternate particular visions of this daily struggle that emerge, such as *mulatez*.

Mestizaje as a Focus on Particularity

Like Elizondo, Isasi-Díaz discusses the primacy of *mestizaje*; it is the basis for her study and the *locus theologicus* of her work.[1] She seeks to come to terms with *mestizaje*, but more precisely from her Cuban experience, which is a variant perspective from that of Virgilio Elizondo. For example, Cuba faced a similar historical mixing of races, ethnicities, and cultures as colonial Mexico. However, there were also differences to the *mestizaje* experienced in Mexico or that which Elizondo described.

Isasi-Díaz recognizes this difference, and as such, she contributes to the discussion by introducing those who may be outside the scope of Elizondo's discussion. She creates room for our awareness and inclusion of those who may have been left out of the original discussion of *mestizaje*. For instance, Cuba was a center for the influx of African slaves to the Americas. This history created an experience quite distinct to that of Elizondo's understanding of the Mexican–American community. Isasi-Díaz thus enters into the theological fray with another alternative to *mestizaje* through the usage of *mulatez*.

Expanding Ethnic and Racial Particularity: *Mulatez*

Mulatez is also an important theological term because it introduces the African experience to the Hispanic theological task. According to the *Diccionario de la Real Academia Española*, the word *mulato* comes

---

[1] Isasi-Díaz, *En la Lucha*, p. 64.

from the Arabic *muwallad*. In the original Arabic it simply means, a person of a mixed race. Perhaps because of its association with Arabic and the Moors who invaded the Iberian Peninsula from Africa the term has come to denote quite exclusively the mixture of whites and blacks. Other authors such as Miguel De La Torre make connections through Portuguese to a racist comparison to a mule. A *mulato* is portrayed as an undomesticated or inferior person.[2]

Because of her particular immigration to the US as well as the experience of racial exclusion that people of African descent have experienced in the US, Isasi-Díaz is sensitive to Afro-Latinos. For our discussion, it first raises the need for awareness of divergent experiences in the US Latino community. Second, it reveals the need to keep in check a drive for the totalization of *mestizaje*. In this we may avoid the systematic razing of the other when it comes to a Latino experience. A discussion on *mestizaje* must include the African experience that characterizes a significant portion of the Latino community in the US. This awareness also suggests further qualification of the term *mestizaje* because one must be aware of the Amerindians from Latin America, as well as other Latin Americans in their midst who have no semblance of whiteness. It will later lead to a more critical look at *mestizaje*, and help us engage in a postcolonial dialogue with world-traveling hybridity.

Expanding Gender Particularity: *Mujerista, Supervivencia,* and *Lo Cotidiano*

Not only does Isasi-Díaz introduce *mulatez* but she also explores the issue of *lo cotidiano*. Lo cotidiano means the visceral reality, and is used to refer to the everyday stuff of life. For Isasi-Díaz, *mestizaje* and *mulatez* always imply the legacy of colonialism as well as the existence under a dominant Eurocentric culture in the US. For such reasons, Isasi-Díaz believes Latinos are primarily concerned about *supervivencia*, or the struggle for survival.[3] This struggle is one in which they must come to terms with and understand their history, the racial categories of *mestizaje* and *mulatez*, and other ongoing *mestizajes* as Latinos in the US.

---

[2] Miguel A. De La Torre, 'Rethinking Mulatez', p. 162.
[3] Isasi-Díaz, *En la Lucha*, pp. 29-30.

To support such a statement Isasi-Díaz addresses the socioeconomic reality of Latinos.[4] She gives hard facts and statistics describing the existence of Latinos on the very margins of North-American society. For instance, they have the highest high-school dropout rate and the lowest education for all ethnic groups in the US.[5] They are also always consistently placed in the lowest end of the economic scale in the US.

These tendencies have not changed. If one thing remains constant for the US Latino community, it is their permanence on the lowest echelons of society. Only 9% of first-generation immigrants are college graduates.[6] The High School dropout rate is twice as high as non-Hispanic whites.[7] In fact, the dropout rate from 1990 to 2000 increased from 32% to 38.1%.[8] Of foreign-born Latinos, 37% made less than $39,000 per year, while 59% of native-born Latinos made less than $39,000 per year.[9]

Hence, theology for Latinos has its center for reflection within the context of *sobrevivencia/supervivencia*. US Latinos are always *en la lucha* (in the struggle) to survive. Concomitantly, the material for theology is *lo cotidiano* (the visceral or common every day stuff).[10] It is for such reasons that Isasi-Díaz turned to ethnographic research to write about *mujerista* theology. In doing so, she affirmed the experiences of women in the Latino community. In her own way she rescued Latinas' daily experiences from the category of the unimportant.[11]

Her method consists of entering the lives of the marginalized. For, Isasi-Díaz, this turns to a purposeful reflection on Latino Women. According to Isasi-Díaz, Hispanic women are always the most exploited members of society: 'La mujer hispana lucha contra el racismo, prejuicio étnico, ligada a la lucha por salvar la cultura

---

[4] Isasi-Díaz, *En la Lucha*, p. 30.

[5] Isasi-Díaz, *En la Lucha*, p. 30.

[6] Daniel R. Sánchez, *Hispanic Realities Impacting America* (Fort Worth, TX: Church Starting Network, 2006), p. 29.

[7] Sánchez, *Hispanic Realities Impacting America*, p. 31.

[8] Sánchez, *Hispanic Realities Impacting America*, p. 32.

[9] Sánchez, *Hispanic Realities Impacting America*, p. 46.

[10] Ada María Isasi-Díaz, *Mujerista Theology: A Theology for the Twenty-first Century* (Maryknoll, NY: Orbis Books, 1996), p. 67.

[11] Isasi-Díaz, *Mujerista Theology*, p. 68.

hispana'.[12] Furthermore, Hispanic women end up on the lowest level of society for multiple reasons: racial, ethnic, and sexist.

> The result of all this is the multifaceded oppression present in the life of Latino women. But they don't give up. They struggle against oppression and their will is not broken in the face of prejudices against them in US society and in their own culture.[13]

Mestizaje and the Movement beyond Particularity to Mutuality

Isasi-Díaz's understanding of *mestizaje* concerning the variety within Latinos in the US is important for this discussion. She first introduced the term *mulatez* thereby expanding the idea of diversity. However, she also discusses the diversity according to country of origin highlighting the tensions between particularity and collectivity of the Latino communities in the US and the complexity of the term *mestizaje*. In her text, *En la Lucha*, she expands on Elizondo who for specific reasons focuses on the Mexican–American reality. She addresses three particular groups: Mexican–Americans, Puerto Ricans, and Cubans. She describes similarities, but Isasi-Díaz is also preoccupied with recognizing the uniqueness of each specific group with unique experiences related to each one. Whereas Elizondo focuses only on Mexican–Americans, Isasi Díaz moves towards a greater awareness of the complexity of the Latino peoples in the US. She also later states that this preoccupation with particularity and specificity is not antithetical to *mestizaje* but required for it to exist.[14] In such a move, her understanding of *mestizaje* uses the colonial past to inform the theological discourse. It also continues to affirm the role of *mestizaje* in the community as they participate in mainstream culture in the US.

In other words, her understanding of *mestizaje* seems to be that in recognizing the particularities of each race, nation, and/or ethnicity of origin using Mexican–American, Cuban, or Puerto Rican realities there can be a greater understanding of how these particularities contribute to the whole of Latino peoples in the US. By fo-

---

[12] Isasi-Díaz, *En la Lucha*, p. 30.

[13] Isasi-Díaz, *En la Lucha*, p. 31.

[14] Isasi-Díaz, *En la Lucha*, p. 190.

cusing on *lo cotidiano*, she begins to look at particular visions of the daily struggle. Politically this dyad of specificity and universality are a great strength. We stand together, yet also may affirm our differences. Her examination of *mestizaje-mulatez* opens the door for other Latin American groups such as Amerindians and *zambos* to be included at the theological roundtable. She informs the theological task by reflecting on *metizaje* as a movement between solidarity and mutuality.[15] One must move away from disinterest towards responsibility and interest toward the other. Although she does not explicitly state so, Isasi-Díaz raises a tension between a specific identity and alternate identities or what I term as *identidad* and *otredad*, an *encuentro* between the self and the other.

In this text she explains her changing self-understanding when it comes to ethnic identity. She shifted in her mindset from being exclusively Cuban to being Cuban-Hispanic. She learned that her particular group is but one piece in the larger Latino body in the US. As such, it deserves necessary particular attention but at the same time it may contribute to the whole. Similarly, the whole may contribute to a particular self-understanding because that self-understanding as Mexican–American, Cuban, or Puerto Rican never speaks exhaustively for the whole.

It is necessary, then, to study the great variety of nations, cultures, races, and ethnicities that include Latinos, giving special attention to categories that are missing from current theological discussion. For example, Central Americans and South Americans deserve significant study. We must examine these in order to provide an understanding of the wide variety of Latino peoples that are included in the whole. Isasi-Díaz states, 'Somos como café con leche: unas más café, otras más leche'.[16] She also states: 'La clase de mestizaje que la teología mujerista abraza es un mestizaje que no resulta en la opresión de una raza por otra. Tiene que ver con la mezcla de culturas africanas, amerindias, y la cultura española.'[17] Her understanding of *mestizaje* must look at the totality of cultures and people groups in Latin America in order for these to gain the self-awareness and understanding required to continue to make theological contribu-

---

[15] Isasi-Díaz, *Mujerista Theology*, p. 89.

[16] Isasi-Díaz, *En la Lucha*, p. 30.

[17] Isasi-Díaz, *En la Lucha*, p. 30, 'We are like coffee with milk: some are more coffee and some are more milk'.

tions. Consequently, there must be a sense of solidarity and mutuality in the relationship between these cultures. There is always a dialogue between the general and specific, between one's identity and the other, or between what we see emerging as *identidad* and *otredad*.

Contributions of Isasi-Díaz's Work

Mestizaje, as Isasi-Díaz describes it, serves as 'the outstanding paradigm and hermeneutical tool' for Latino and *mujerista* theological praxis.[18] It is also a symbol of these communities, and furthermore a symbol of Latinas' moral truth-praxis because it is grounded in *lo cotidiano* (the daily struggle).[19] These are strong statements to make, as Isasi-Díaz is indeed conscious the complexity of colonialism and the formation of Latin America; thus, she is using *mestizaje* as the locus to describe the mixing and colonial past of Latin America as the starting point and the most essential element, or locus, of US Latino theology.

Furthermore, she states that *mestizaje* should not be an abstraction of the past but a present historical reality being processed and worked out in the reality of the people.[20] Consequently, this stance must be affirmed and chosen repeatedly in all dimensions of theology, because *mestizaje* must include an expression of responsibility for each other.[21] Mutuality is essential in the sense that there must be a responsibility for understanding and working together in the context of communality and interrelationships. She states, 'No nos podemos salvar a costa de nadie, ni en forma individual, dejando a las otras detrás'.[22] Therefore, *mestizaje* must be thoroughly mindful of the totality of the Latino community, and reminds us that we are not isolated individuals or nationalities; consequently, we cannot leave anyone behind, much less become the oppressors ourselves.

Isasi-Díaz states that Hispanics must critique and denounce oppressive structures in society while at the same time refuse to ro-

---

18 Isasi-Díaz, *En la Lucha*, p. 195.

19 Isasi-Díaz, *En la Lucha*, p. 196.

20 Isasi-Díaz, *En la Lucha*, p. 196.

21 Isasi-Díaz, *En la Lucha*, p. 198.

22 Isasi-Díaz, *En la Lucha*, p. 30, 'We cannot save ourselves in spite of others, especially not in an individual form leaving others behind'.

manticize Latino culture.[23] This means that the term *mestizaje* must understand the Hispanic situation as oppressed peoples. The danger is to absorb the term *mestizaje* uncritically. Isasi-Díaz is much more aware of the need for the term to be more nuanced. Hispanics must come to terms with their history and theological vocation in order to struggle against oppression manifested through domination, subjugation, exploitation, and repression – the colonial legacy – through a liberative project.

Her perspective on women is one example of how not to romanticize Latino culture. One of her strongest critiques of Latino culture is the staunch *machismo* (male chauvinism) that affects women negatively. Also, this leads us to seek to understand the plight of immigrant women and their families who make the journey *al norte*. Many of these women are some of the most oppressed persons along the US-Mexico border. There are many articles that raise awareness on how many of them end up working as sex slaves in cities along the journey.[24]

Limitations of Isasi-Díaz's Work

There are still some general considerations that may prove to be problematic for continued discussion with those from Latin America. In scholarship there is a general omission of the other immigrants to the US: Central Americans and/or South Americans. This is the case in her theology. Perhaps this has to do with the fact that many come here to work and do not have the privilege to study and consequently do not make themselves known in the Academy. There is also the omission of other racial and ethnic identities in Latin America, such as Amerindian realities. There is much more

---

[23] Isasi-Díaz, *En la Lucha*, pp. 170-71.

[24] See Raúl Zaldívar, '*El Rostro de un Pueblo Sufrido*', in Miguel Álvarez, David Ramírez, and Raúl Zaldívar (eds.), *El Rostro Hispano de Jesús* (Chicago: *Universidad para Líderes*, 2009), pp. 17-98 (p. 54). Departamento 19, 'Migrantes Hondureños en los Ojos de los Carteles' http://departamento19.hn/index.php/portada/69/6859.html (accessed August 14, 2012). María Peters, 'Hondureñas Se Convierten en Esclavas Sexuales en Mexico', *El Heraldo* http://www.elheraldo.hn/Secciones-Principales/Al-Frente/Hondurenas-esclavas-sexuales-en-Mexico (accessed September 3, 2012).

discussion that can potentially take place in this regard and we are touching a small dimension of this potentiality.

Nonetheless, Ada María Isasi-Díaz moved the discussion in the right direction. However, in order to complete her project toward a Latino self-understanding each separate nation, racial category, ethnicity, and culture from Latin America must be allowed to make a contribution to enrich the understanding of *mestizaje* and in turn the self-understanding of the US Latino community. The goal is that we not only discuss a single monolithic US Latino community but several diverse Latino communities in the US.

For instance, we could discuss Salvadorans, Guatemalans, Nicaraguans, or Hondurans. These nations are similar in many ways yet they are distinct in several other ways. Even within these countries there are a great variety of ethnic, racial, and cultural groups that must be recognized for who they are. In the case of Honduras, one has to deal with *indio*, *mestizo*, *mulato*, and *zambo* realities. Such is the case of the *Lencas*, *Chortís*, *Pech*, *Tawahks*, *Tolupanes*, *Miskitos*, *Africanos*, and *Garífunas* present in the country and also present in the US along with *mestizo* and *mulato* peoples. There are also Arab, Chinese, Palestinian, and other realities in all of Latin America who have experienced their own *mestizajes*. Some of these wield a lot of power because they immigrated with resources to invest in businesses in these countries.[25]

Furthermore, there must be more study of undocumented immigration and the realities these immigrants face. It is an omission that we must be ready to take into account today especially in light of the politicization of undocumented immigration, and because it is an opportunity to use *lo cotidiano* as the source of theological reflection. Undocumented immigrants are a dimension that must be included in Isasi-Díaz's understanding of *lo cotidiano* in Latino lives, especially with some estimates putting the number at around 7 to 12 million in the US. Because *mestizaje* refers to mixtures, it is essential that we do not isolate ourselves and use our quest to dwell in *mestizaje*, thereby remaining closed to the other in our theology. Nonetheless, I shall follow her example in this work, insisting that the

---

[25] Jeffrey W. Bentley, 'Honduras', in Melvin Ember and Carol R. Emer (eds.), *Countries and their Cultures* (NY: Macmillan Ref., 2001), II, pp. 979-90 (p. 981).

material for doing theology from a Latino reality comes precisely from *lo cotidiano*.

Conclusions from Isasi-Díaz

In this chapter I highlighted the theology of Ada María Isasi-Díaz. She makes further contributions to Elizondo's by developing a theology of mutuality and solidarity that takes into consideration a more expansive understanding of *mestizaje* derived from other racial and ethnic mixes through *mulatez*, the daily struggle for life in *lo coditiano*, and women through *mujerista* theology. She sees subtexts and mixes beyond *mestizaje*, and thus may point the way to a possible connection toward a transcultural *hibridez* inherent to the Latino communities in the US. *Mujerista* theology and *mulatez* are ideas that resist cultural assimilation and acculturation but demonstrate the need for an awareness of the other. Thus, she begins to demonstrate a tension between *identidad* and *otredad*.

Furthermore, Isasi-Díaz expands the material for discussion in many ways. She makes us aware of a *cosmovisión* based on *supervivencia*. There are alternate particular visions of this daily struggle that emerge such as *mulatez* and other realities. She is an example of a positive contribution building upon the principle of *mestizaje*. She described three dimensions, Puerto Rican, Cuban, and Mexican. However, as we have said, there are many more nationalities and cultural groups present in the US. There are also distinct *mujerista* perspectives.

Elizondo's and Isasi-Díaz's work on *mestizaje* reveals the importance of this term in the way it informs theological reflection. It establishes an understanding for the Latino peoples in the US while revealing the need for further investigation and discussion on these issues.

The analysis of *mestizaje* cannot be neutral. It calls theology to be grounded in and engaged in the daily struggles of Hispanics/Latin@s for survival. *Mestizaje* serves as the outstanding paradigm and hermeneutical tool for Hispanics/Latin@s and *mujerista* theological praxis. It is also a symbol of these communities, and furthermore a theology grounded in *lo cotidiano*. Isasi-Díaz moves forward from Elizondo as he states that Hispanics must critique and denounce oppressive structures in society while refusing to romanticize Latino culture.

Isasi-Díaz's work on *mestizaje*, however, also needs to be expanded in other areas. There is no mention of undocumented immigration and/or the realities these immigrants face. This is an area full of potential as she mentions *lo cotidiano* as the source of theological reflection. One final dimension is explaining theologically the relationship between *identidad* and *otredad*. We must engage theology to produce a just praxis and a relationality that is oriented after God's Kingdom. Nonetheless, at this point we must consider more recent theological reflection on *mestizaje* and the continued nuances that have surged from reflection on this term.

4

SECULAR CRITIQUES OF *MESTIZAJE*: *MESCOLANZA Y MESTIZAJES*

Introduction

I have explored two major descriptions of *mestizaje*. I note that it has been significant for US Hispanic theologians in that it has served as a theological departure point for Latino peoples. It serves as a useful term to name the collective US Latino peoples, their *cosmovisiones*, and their way of being in the world. It is also a term that points to *supervivencia* and the need to do theology from *lo cotidiano*. An approach such as the one taken by Isasi-Díaz creates the need to understand alternate forms of being Latino. It also reveals that there are particular visions as revealed by the daily struggle of Latinos. This is demonstrated by her use of the terminology *mujerista* and *mulatez*. Finally, her usage reveals the need to engage further these concepts and articulate these particular visions of the daily struggle. Such an approach could help inform an analysis of undocumented immigration.

For this study, *mestizaje* points toward the rich variety of interrelationships in the Latino community and the people of Latin America. Nonetheless, there remain some tensions in *mestizaje* that demand further attention. For example, tensions remain in defining the relationship between a particular specific identity and the collective whole that this term tries to encapsulate. Also, there are formulations of the relationship between *mestizaje* and *mulatez* that could potentially merge the two uncritically without giving much thought to alternate Latin American meanings of the term. An example is that of a Honduran living among Puerto Ricans and Mexicans in Brooklyn, NY. He or she has to learn not only American culture, but the cultures of these fellow Spanish-speakers. There is culture shock among these fellow Latinos, from humor to culinary preference.

In this chapter I further elucidate these tensions by observing how *mestizaje* may unravel and become a complicated and slippery concept. Nonetheless, I wish to demonstrate that it still points to a relationship of *identidad* and *otredad* and ultimately reveals a transcultural reality best identified as an *hibridez latina* that points towards the need of understanding multiple *cosmovisiones*. This step helps to enrich a Latino self-understanding. We must look at differing realities if we are to talk of a shared identity and if we are to discuss the plight of undocumented immigrants.

Critiques of *Mestizaje*

I turn to perspectives differing from a Roman Catholic point-of-view because several authors strongly criticize the US Latino conceptions of *mestizaje*. In this particular chapter I take a look at Manuel Vásquez's analysis of *mestizaje*. He is a social theorist that has heavily criticized Latino notions of *mestizaje*. I also look at Miguel De La Torre, an ethicist and a theologian, as another author that has offered a critique on the formulations of *mulatez*. These critiques serve to give another insight into the world of immigrants from Latin America and the need to consider the variant Latin American perspectives. I close with a look at Néstor Medina, a Latino Theologian who has produced the most definitive work on *mestizaje* to date. These authors demonstrate continued engagement from *mestizaje* to variant experiences in Latin America.

Manuel A. Vásquez: A Central American Experience

Manuel Vásquez is a professor in the Department of Religion at the University of Florida. He is an author concerned with the religions of Latin America and among US Latinos. His area of expertise is the intersection of religion, immigration, and globalization in the Americas. Among other interests he is developing a comparison on contemporary transnational Latin American and African religious networks. Furthermore, he is interested in method and theory in the study of religion, particularly in issues connected with embodiment, material culture, practice, place-making, and mobility.[1]

His particular perspective is important as it demonstrates an emerging awareness from authors from backgrounds other than Puerto Rico, Cuba, and Mexico who have contributed to the dialogue of *mestizaje* as a pan-Latino reality. Vásquez is from El Salvador; and, as such, he discusses *mestizaje* from his particular Central American perspective.

Vásquez finds many positive things in the concept of *mestizaje* claiming it is indeed the core paradigm in Latino Theology.[2] However, he strongly critiques the current usage of the term. His particular vantage point leads him to question whether or not this term elucidates the diversity within Latino people, and whether it explains power asymmetries that exclude and divide *within* Latinos themselves.[3] His concern is not only the relationship to the dominant culture, but also the relationship within the Latino communities. Furthermore, he warns readers that when *mestizaje* is not used properly it can be an exclusionary, ethnocentric, and racist term disguised as an inclusionary term. For these reasons, Vásquez calls for a more nuanced understanding of *mestizaje*.

A Heavy Critique of *Mestizaje*

Vásquez strongly critiques the usage of *mestizaje*. First, he describes how *mestizaje* is currently being used generally to describe Central and South Americans, a region covering over 20 different countries. Vásquez explains that each of these nations has its own history and that this demarcation covers equally diverse peoples and cultures. Such diversity prompts him to question this universal and totalizing implementation of the term *mestizaje*.

Vásquez also describes his journey in El Salvador, a country with an unfortunate and painful history of violence. In this nation the term *mestizo* was used as a grand metanarrative to excuse violence against *campesinos*, *amerindios*, women, and the poor in order to build

---

[1] 'Manuel Vásquez', by the University of Florida, http://web.religion.ufl.edu/faculty/vasquez.html (accessed April 11, 2012).

[2] Manuel A. Vásquez, 'Rethinking *Mestizaje*', in De La Torre and Espinosa (eds.) *Rethinking Latino(a) Religion and Identity*, pp. 129-57 (p. 129).

[3] Vásquez, 'Rethinking *Mestizaje*', p. 130.

a unified nation. Vásquez describes this violence with his case-in-point being *La Matanza de 1932* in which the military massacred 10,000 *campesinos* (most of indigenous descent) in order to bring order to a chaotic nation-state. In the years that followed the massacre an extreme form of violence ensued that led thousands to immigrate to the US and other countries. This violence reached its apex with two deplorable incidents: the assassination of Archbishop Romero while giving mass on March 24, 1980, and the rape and murder of six Roman Catholic nuns on December 2, 1980.

Vásquez argues that we need to be careful in implementing *mestizaje*. His reason is that from the period of *La Matanza* to the end of the 20th century *mestizaje* was used as an educational tool to explain that El Salvador was a *mestizo* (emphasis on masculinity here) nation. Thus, the ideal Salvadoran was a male person mixed with whiteness. Consequently, the military *junta's* task became to wipe out *campesinos* and *indígenas* in order to build this *mestizo* nation. Vásquez states, '*mestizaje* functioned as the nation-building myth that has helped link dark to light-skinned hybrids and Euro-Americans, often in opposition to both foreigners and indigenous others in their midst'.[4] Like similar terms that have been used in a generalizing manner, there is always an inherent danger that *mestizaje* may also become racist and exclusivist. At its worst there is the fear that it may become violent as peoples try to whiten themselves in order to position themselves for social power and control as they compete against one another.

With such an example, Vásquez resists idealizing the term because 'it falsifies in the most drastic manner the condition of our [Latino or Latin American] culture and literature'.[5] Vásquez observes a problem when universalizing the term precisely because Latinos are extremely diverse, racially and ethnically. Thus, *mestizaje* reveals an inherent contradiction because it calls for a common Latino identity at the expense of forcibly harmonizing Latinos. Vásquez argues that these are much more fragmented and diverse than is perceived. He also creates a movement of resistance towards cultural assimilation and acculturation because the particularities of each of these groups cannot be subsumed or lost in their interactions with each other. Many of these tensions remain ecclesiastically

---

[4] Vásquez, 'Rethinking *Mestizaje*', p. 145.

[5] Vásquez, 'Rethinking *Mestizaje*', p. 144.

because of ethnocentric tensions where some nationalities look at others as inferior sometimes just because of a difference in regional accent of spoken Spanish. Sometimes in the case of immigrants there may be a hierarchical division and positioning between those who 'have papers' and those who do not, or those who speak English and those who do not.

For Vásquez in the case of El Salvador, the term *mestizo* served the interests of the powerful and elite. These wanted to create smooth and conflict-free spaces of coexistence by force.[6] As a consequence, the elite used this term as a concept to raze their opposition. *Mestizaje*, as articulated by elites, promoted amnesia in conscience concerning the violence towards and the continued suffering of the poor and indigenous peoples of Latin America.[7]

For Vásquez, *mestizo* in El Salvador meant whiteness, power, *machismo*, and progress in the name of building a nation, which resulted in a dichotomy in peoples' conscience. To be *indio* or darker-skinned meant that one was impotent, primitive, and was associated with a tribal mentality.[8] Similarly, calling someone an *indio* is considered an insult in my native Honduras, whereas in Puerto Rico being called an *indio* is a compliment.

Vásquez explains how several communities in Central America become marginalized because they cannot call themselves *mestizos*, such as the Mayans in Guatemala.[9] Vásquez suggests that because they have little or no European roots, they experience a *ningunidad* or nothingness.[10] They are left out of political, community, and economic projects for the elite. Consequently, a danger in using this terminology is that it may delegitimize and exclude native peoples, non-whites, and the poor. Vásquez is even suspicious of this term as used by postcolonial theologians because he thinks it promotes racism as well as political and economic exclusion for non-white peoples. In Honduras in 2015, for example, there was a scandal where the ruling political party stole an estimated $200 million dol-

---

[6] Vásquez, 'Rethinking *Mestizaje*', p. 144.

[7] Vásquez, 'Rethinking *Mestizaje*', p. 145.

[8] Vásquez, 'Rethinking *Mestizaje*', p. 145

[9] Vásquez, 'Rethinking *Mestizaje*', p. 148.

[10] Vásquez, 'Rethinking Mestizaje' p. 148. *Ladino* is a term that is used interchangeably with *mestizo*. It refers to the dominant people group of these nations that are more heavily influenced by Iberean ideals.

lars from the *Instituto Hondureño de Seguro Social*. The organization went bankrupt. Many poor people died because of a lack of medicines. None of the masterminds of this scheme have faced the justice system.

To summarize, Vásquez's concern is that *mestizaje* leaves itself open to masked drives toward totalization and homogenization, no matter how much in-betweenness and border-crossings are celebrated.[11] Therefore, he makes the following claim: *mestizaje* is a viable metaphor only if it is historicized, contextualized, relativized, and confronted with the otherness that it contains and fails to contain.[12] There must be a dynamic movement when discussing *mestizaje* between the identity of a particular group or a particular self-understanding and otherness, between *identidad* and *otredad*, or one's identity and the irreconcilable other. One must also recognize the progressive and evolving nature of culture in order to be free from imprisoning or oppressive hegemonic tendencies.

Moving Beyond Tribalism

While Vásquez nearly jettisons the term, he concludes that *mestizaje* is still useful because it reflects *lo cotidiano*. Furthermore, *mestizaje* opens the door to critique the bipolar racial formation in the US that seems to be conscious only of black versus white, and which sees Latinos as inferior in race hierarchies. He also sees that it is a useful term to critique the post 9/11 world, especially in its angry rhetoric towards undocumented immigrants.[13] It may lead to understanding this condition and explaining the reasons why these immigrants choose to live in such conditions.

Vásquez's main point is that theologians must be mindful of the epistemological violence we commit when we speak for, about, and to our communities.[14] He points to a tension between representing and being represented, between what others have observed through *darstellen* and *verstellen* (speaking for and speaking about the communities).[15] He calls for respect towards the other and to resist descriptions that violate the diverse peoples of Latin America, for these are

---

[11] Vásquez, 'Rethinking *Mestizaje*', p. 149.

[12] Vásquez, 'Rethinking *Mestizaje*', p. 149

[13] Vásquez, 'Rethinking *Mestizaje*', pp. 151-52.

[14] Vásquez, 'Rethinking *Mestizaje*', p. 152.

[15] Anjali Prabhu, *Hybridity: Limits, Transformations, Prospects* (Albany: SUNY Press, 2007), p. 12.

peoples that do not fit neatly into our created categories. For Vásquez, to avoid reducing them in our descriptions we must always be aware of the other.[16] This is especially relevant in the US as laws oversimplify the complexity of undocumented immigration or do not give consideration to such complexities. It becomes especially important to realize that not all Hispanic people have had the same experiences. Each has some kind of contribution to make in the US.

I also think that for the poor, the immigration system is unjust. Those who need to immigrate must pay an exorbitant fee to go to the US embassy. They must furthermore prove they have an education, own property, and have a lot of money in their bank accounts. By contrast, the reality is that most people who need to immigrate are chronically poor, do not have money, and cannot even afford to pay the embassy fee. The US embassy is only for the rich, and the majority of the people in the country are *en la lucha por supervivencia.*

Balancing *Mestizaje* and *Otredad*

Vásquez admits that the inherent danger of his critique is trying to conceive the other as empty space or as an inaccessible blankness.[17] The other is not simply an unreadable text or an absence endlessly caught in a sign system.[18] Conversely, Vásquez writes that the other is an embodied and historical individual that is constituted not only by subjectivizing discourses and practices of nation-states, but also by his or her own creative work upon the fragments of the colonial legacy. He also calls this a viscerality of the *other* grounded in *lo cotidiano* which provides a starting point for examining *the other*. In such a statement, Vásquez also avoids a semiotic reductionism and recognizes the material presence or *lo cotidiano* (viscerality) of the other.

For our discussion of *mestizaje*, he preserves both a sense of independence and unknowability for the other as well as the reality and viscerality of the other in order to move forward. Though unknowable, Vásquez still presents identity as fluid and relational thereby open to change and opening the possibility for understanding. He challenges Western essentialism and obsession with fixed

---

[16] Vásquez, 'Rethinking *Mestizaje*', p. 153.

[17] Vásquez, 'Rethinking *Mestizaje*', p. 154.

[18] Vásquez, 'Rethinking *Mestizaje*', p. 154.

boundaries, particularly with hierarchical binarianism of Black-White. For these reasons, Vásquez does not do away with *mestizaje*; rather, he suggests we build an intra-ethnic solidarity based on *mestizaje's* de-centering of self and a world-traveling that *hibridity* encourages.[19] It is here that I think we may be able to discuss hybridity and an emerging Latino *hibridez* that may aid our discussion of *mestizaje* to include the ultimate *other* – undocumented immigrants to the US. I also think that to understand *mestizaje* and make it more nuanced we must also look at postcolonial writings on hybridity as these may help us understand and qualify an emerging *hibridez*.

Vásquez reinforces the notion that Hispanics are people living in tension between with binding similarities and unavoidable differences.[20] The locus of Latino theology is not just *mestizaje* but the tense relationship between *mescolanza* and *otredad*. Any vision of *mestizaje* must be inclusive of this tension. Vásquez seeks to include other races, cultures, and people groups that may not be included by *mestizaje* or *mulatez* but are, nonetheless, part of a US Latino community. This is in tune with Isasi-Díaz's movement to recognize the particularity and the collectiveness of Latinos in the theological task, and with Elizondo's back and forth movements or exchanges between the peoples and cultures experiencing *mestizaje*.

A Critique of Vásquez

While Vásquez has opened the door to those that do not necessarily fit in the categories, his critique is problematic. *Mestizaje* is in danger of becoming a concept that merely describes racial markers. As we have seen, *mestizaje* is concerned with the state-of-being of Latino peoples and to the community's *cosmovisión* or *cosmovisiones*. The question of existence in the US always introduces the question of race versus ethnicity. While these may be interwoven, they can also exist apart from each other. Race always inserts a challenge as it is a dimension with several shortcomings in North American as well as in Latin American history.

Another problem in Vásquez is the inclusion of *mescolanza* in the discussion of *metizaje*. The *Diccionario de la Real Academia Española* explains that in Spanish this term may connote something strange or confusing: 'Mezcla extraña y confusa, y algunas veces ridícula'. It

---

[19] Vásquez, 'Rethinking *Mestizaje*', p. 155.
[20] Vásquez, 'Rethinking *Mestizaje*', p. 155.

is similar to the sense that 'motley' conveys in English. This may be problematic because such connotations may make it another extremely pejorative term. Nonetheless, in light of the life of the poor, marginalized, and oppressed in Latin America, it may be a vivid portrayal of their lives. More work must be done to describe this *mescolanza*. Lastly, Latino theologians have used *mestizaje* extensively, repeatedly calling it the *locus theologicus* of their theology. Therefore, it may be problematic to jettison the term.

Conclusions on Vásquez

At this point, we could take a step back and leave *mestizaje* as one category within a general Latino framework. There is room for *mulatez, mujerismo*, and other alternate realities. I suggest this framework is a pan-Hispanic or pan-Latino reality, or a collective Latino reality characterized by what Vásquez has called a world traveling hybridity.[21] However, *hibridez* is also useful as a necessary component of *mestizaje* in order to continue discussing a general Latino framework. Characterizing this *hibridez* is the tension between *identidad* and *otredad*. *Hibridez* calls for dialogue within and with those outside the community and with other Latino theologians along with the *concientización* gathered from divergent voices within this collective whole. In trying to name this reality we may be able to retain the sense of uniqueness concerning this historical intermixture that characterizes the collective Latino community.

For example, I pastored in New York City for seven years as I was writing this study. My parishioners lived and carried out their lives in relationship with a majority African-American community. These parishioners, adults and children, took on a lot of African-American cultural traits. The youth, especially, were socialized from preschool to high school in a majority African-American world. This produced interesting mixtures that did not neatly remain a *mestizaje*, but seemed more like a new thing altogether. It was an *hibridez* from *mestizaje* to African-American culture.

Such an example highlights that our discussion on *mestizaje* as the *locus theologicus* of Latinos is caught in a dialogue between identity and otherness, between *identidad* and *otredad*. Thus, theologians must 'create alternative ways for conceiving and articulating the experi-

---

[21] Vásquez, 'Rethinking *Mestizaje*', p. 155.

ences and identities coexisting among Latino communities'.[22] In Vásquez's critique there is a strong sense of an interrelationship between mixtures that *mestizaje* implies. There is always a tension between two identities that cannot be collapsed. This is the idea of *identidad* and *otredad*. These two go hand in hand. They reach towards fellow Latinos and beyond these towards non-Latinos. Vásquez points the way toward understanding other Latinos and other racial, cultural, and ethnic groups that may not be included by *mestizaje*, but are nonetheless part of Latino communities. This also opens the door to the discussion of those overlooked on the margins: *mulato*, undocumented immigrants, Amerindian, *zambo* and other peoples who have bordered *mestizo* realities.

Miguel A. De La Torre: an Alternate Vision in *Mulatez*

We must also discuss *mulatez* when describing *mestizaje* because it reveals several tensions within the collective identity of Latino peoples. Miguel De La Torre offers a similar criticism as Vásquez when discussing *mulatez*. De La Torre is Professor of Social Ethics at the Iliff School of Theology in Denver, an institution that claims a liberal Christian heritage and is committed to being a leader in diversity in theological education. His particular reading of *mulatez* is a strong critique against it.

De La Torre's main problem with *mulatez* is that it masks internal Hispanic racism.[23] Also, it reveals intra-Latino structures of oppression. He remains concerned about the usage of *mulatez* because those claiming to be *mulatos* may use it to mask claims to power and/or privilege. As in the case of *mestizaje*, *mulatez* is a concept that whitens blacks; those with access to whiteness may claim power and privilege. There is much historical baggage with which the collective identity has to deal including such cultural sayings like: *hay que mejorar la raza*.

De La Torre lists more concerns in using the term *mulato*. First, De La Torre believes it links a biracial Hispanic with an animal, the mule (*mulo/mula*).[24] Again, in Portuguese *mulato* signifies derision as

---

[22] Medina, *Mestizaje*, p. 107.
[23] De La Torre, 'Rethinking *Mulatez*', p. 159.
[24] De La Torre, 'Rethinking *Mulatez*', p. 162.

it is used to speak about a mule or those people without domesticity. De La Torre argues that one cannot escape this negative connotation when using it.[25] Moreover, he continues to claim one cannot escape the hidden meaning to whiten Africans, which is a violent act.

According to De La Torre, while *mestizaje* is caught in a colonizing discourse against indigenous people, *mulatez* connotes a perspective of social and economic genocide of those of African descent by erasing the black race and whitening it.[26] Thus, De La Torre cautions against using *mulatez* as a symbol for lifting supposedly savage races toward civilization and progress because it makes *blanqueamiento* or whitening, a prerequisite for black advancement.

De La Torre's critique is probably the most poignant for this discussion of *mestizaje*. The reason is that Africans and people of African descent have suffered many injustices due to the colonial legacy. Nonetheless, the main problem with De La Torre is that it seems impossible to celebrate *mulatez*. Even in his description, he reduces *mulatez* to a completely negative rendering of the African experience in the Americas.

A Critique of De La Torre
In sharp contrast to De La Torre, I think the term may be rescued and used in a positive manner. Though the usage of *mulatez* in De La Torre seems beyond rescue there is another dimension contained in this term that may be full of life and meaning. De La Torre does not suggest any other term that can be used to describe this history and fails to bring life to this reality – especially since some consciously choose *mulatez* as their own identity and can be fulfilled in both their African heritage as well as in their European heritage. Furthermore, De La Torre's critique reduces this issue of identity to a matter of racial categories. Previous authors have suggested that this is a matter beyond a discussion on race. It deals with *cosmovisión* and interrelationships in forming an identity.

The other critique of De La Torre is that this term has its own history. It must be included alongside *mestizaje*. This puts *mestizaje* and *mulatez* both in relationship with the other they fail to contain.

---

[25] De La Torre, 'Rethinking *Mulatez*', p. 162.
[26] De La Torre, 'Rethinking *Mulatez*', p. 164.

This movement decenters both and shows an emerging increasingly complex reality characterized by Vásquez's world traveling hybridity.

Conclusions on De La Torre

As negative as De La Torre's critique is, he does state that one cannot write concerning *mulatez* without acknowledging the other in Latino communities. One cannot ignore the history or the suffering of these dimensions in Latino peoples. However, unlike what De La Torre suggests, this term does not have to remain in a negative and/or racist dimension. Again, his critique radically contrasts with what other authors have stated in the sense that he does not and cannot redeem the *mulato*. De La Torre could have included ways in which to redeem the term and ways to relate this to the discussion concerning *mestizaje*. For example, he could suggest *mulatez* existing as an alternative and legitimate vision in the collective identity of Pan-Latino or even Latin American peoples. He could also describe the positive contributions that *mulatez* has created in the collective identity of Latin American and Latino peoples, which highlights a further dimension in a Latino or even Latin American *hibridez*.

Néstor Medina: *Mestizaj*e-Intermixture

A final author that must be considered is Néstor Medina. Medina is a Guatemalan author who has lived and worked in Canada and has taught at Regent University in Virginia Beach. He arrived at similar conclusions as Vásquez and De La Torre. Again, a thorough critique of Medina's work is beyond the scope of this book, inasmuch as I only want to focus on the aspects of Medina's work that contribute to my proposal of an emerging world traveling hybridity, or *hibridez*.

Medina gives an account of the history of *mestizaje* within the evolving self-understanding of Latino theologians. He also states that *mestizaje* was absorbed uncritically as a way to debunk a white-black discourse in the US. Later on, with critiques from Latin America, US Latino authors became aware of the need to nuance this term. He also admits that there are various problems that the dimensions of race and ethnicity create for a discussion of Latin America. Like De La Torre and Vásquez, he agrees that in Latin

America the problem with *mestizaje* is that it is still used as a term to whiten the population or oneself.[27]

Further Discussion of *Mestizaje*

Medina continues to expand on the discussion by pointing to a gap between US Latino theologians and Latin American reflections. US Latino theologians were unaware of the risks in incorporating *mestizaje* until they started taking Latin American reflections into account. Consequently, Medina affirms what Vásquez and De La Torre have started to describe. It becomes necessary to review articulations of ethnic and cultural identity.[28]

Originally, *mestizaje* revealed the reality of oppression and marginalization in the US. It created a praxis of resistance towards assimilationist tendencies. It also served as the privileged center of theological reflection in the Hispanic community. The term was positive because it allowed the community to reclaim the history of biological and cultural intermixture.[29] However, Medina's claim is that these theologians failed to pay attention to Latin American context and hegemonic expressions of *mestizaje*.[30] Medina even states that US Latino theologians uncritically adopted *mestizaje*. In doing so, these theologians presented a homogenous *mestizo* community when in reality this diversity is much greater than first supposed. Furthermore, Medina states that these communities coexist in varied tensions within US populations.[31] For this reason, theologians must confront challenges and tensions in the theological use of *mestizaje* in light of rapidly changing social and political contexts of the US, especially with criticism from indigenous and African communities.[32]

Concomitantly, Medina believes Latino theologians are even now fashioning new notions and reworking *mestizaje* in their theologies. This means that the future is open for corrections. Medina continues to state that there is no finished *mestizaje*. Furthermore, he offers the alternative of continuing to use the term, but in its plural form, *mestizajes* (underline mine to add emphasis), as a way to de-

---

27 Medina, *Mestizaje*, p. 24.
28 Medina, *Mestizaje*, p. ix.
29 Medina, *Mestizaje*, pp. x-xi.
30 Medina, *Mestizaje*, p. xii.
31 Medina, *Mestizaje*, p. xiii.
32 Medina, *Mestizaje*, p. xiv.

scribe the variety of mixtures that make up Latino peoples. Lastly, his understanding of *mestizajes* must be discussed in light of the historical context out of which it emerges.[33] His purpose is to engage in interreligious and intercultural conversations with different ethnic and cultural traditions. These are conversation partners in the struggle to build a more inclusive society. Medina therefore calls for Latino communities to engage in deeper intra-Latino approaches to theology and to create intra-Latino interreligious conversations.[34]

A Critique: *Mestizajes*

According to Medina, *mestizaje* can become a mechanism of liberation or oppression.[35] This is a tension that we must also highlight here. It has been present throughout this discussion, but Medina is able to name it most effectively. It is a tension between affirming and negating identity. For example, *mestizaje* contains contradictory meanings that can at the same time be recovered from an oppressive meaning to affirm different communities. Simultaneously, it may be utilized as a tool for oppression by excluding others from a specific community. In other words, there are two possible perspectives when dealing with *mestizaje*. The first is *mestizaje*-as-mixture; and the second is *mestizaje*-as-miscegenation. The former connotes its positive dimensions, while the latter its negative dimensions.[36]

Further, *mestizaje* also reveals the challenge of holding in tension particular identity of Latinos with their collective identity.[37] This is the reason that Medina uses the term, *mestizajes*. He avoids collapsing *mestizaje* into a singular slice of identity and prefers the general meaning and connotation of the term: intermixture. Nonetheless, he believes that theologians must retrieve the messy and oppressive history of *mestizaje* in order to disallow the unqualified use of the term.[38] These rearrangements challenge theologians to create alternative ways for conceiving and articulating the experiences and identities coexisting among Latino communities. This opens the door to *the other* in Latino theology. For Medina, this also reveals an

---

[33] Medina, *Mestizaje*, p. xiv.
[34] Medina, *Mestizaje*, p. xvi.
[35] Medina, *Mestizaje*, p. xvii.
[36] Medina, *Mestizaje*, p. 36.
[37] Medina, *Mestizaje*, p. 42.
[38] Medina, *Mestizaje*, p. 43.

ambiguous web of *mestizaje* and heterogeneity.[39] It appears again to be a relationship between *identidad* and *otredad*, characteristics of *hibridez*.

Such reflections open up new material for research, given the marked absence of indigenous and African peoples. This includes seasonal workers, undocumented workers, and new immigrants. It includes differences in generations, as well as those between urban and rural communities. For Medina, it is necessary to acknowledge the diversity of the Latino population outside of synthetic and universalizing notions.[40]

Medina calls this awareness a multiplicity of consciousness, and/or a more complex reality that is *yet to be named*.[41] He also adds that the terminology of borderlands can better evoke a decolonizing emphasis marking the intersections of identities, cultures, consciousness, bodies, and peoples. Medina calls this borderland reality: intermixture-*mestizaje*.[42] This experience becomes a unifying factor for Latin America, as it is always dealing with intermixture. It is an ongoing tension that cannot go away. Intermixture-*mestizaje* appears to be for Medina what other authors seem to describe as an ongoing tension between *identidad* and *otredad*.

Conclusions on Medina's *Mestizajes*

When Medina begins to give content to this reality that theologians have termed *mestizaje*, he describes *mestizajes* as pointing to a multiplicity of consciousness, which he states is a more complex reality that is yet to be named. This means that *mestizaje* retreats from its specificity and claims to capture a common Latino reality, particularly from the vantage point of the oppressed. Again, this is accomplished through the usage of the term, *mestizajes*.

Additionally, this leaves Latino theology with the need to name this reality. However, whatever it is called, it must be aware of the tensions revealed in the preceding studies of *mestizaje*. These theologians appear to describe variant dimensions of the collective Latino reality. This makes *mestizaje* not *the locus theologicus* par excellence, but a *locus theologicus* within Latino theology. Yet within *mestizaje* and

---

[39] Medina, *Mestizaje*, p. 107.
[40] Medina, *Mestizaje*, p. 111.
[41] Medina, *Mestizaje*, p. 134.
[42] Medina, *Mestizaje*, p. 134.

within *mulatez* there are tensions in *identidad* and *otredad* that these terms fail to contain, which leads us to note that Latino communities are marked by fluctuating dimensions of *hibridez* resulting from the *encontronazos* between *identidad* and *otredad* in *lo cotidiano*. These are always evolving and never static. Pigmentocracy, or delineations based solely on race, are never adequate descriptors for the people of Latin American heritage. Medina, as Vásquez and De La Torre, points to the creation of alternate categories that must qualify the use of *mestizaje* or any descriptor of the Latin American peoples who make their journey *al norte*. These are part of an emerging *hibridez* that may include those outside the traditional scope of theology, such as undocumented immigrants.

Conclusion

At this juncture, I summarize this exploration up to this point. First, we have examined different conceptualizations concerning *mestizaje*. The first author we examined was Virgilio Elizondo. He implemented the term *mestizaje* in order to name his community. He moved away from the Black versus White discourse into a discussion that made room for the Latinos in the US. He called for a nuanced understanding of this community in a way that looked at the oppressive history of the term *mestizaje* and at the same time allowed him to recover this messy history to name his community. He also asserts that this term may help describe the Mexican–American *cosmovisión*. Other authors used this same term to apply it from the Mexican–American community to the experience of other Latino communities in the US.

More theologians embraced this term because it provided necessary resistance to an exclusively black-white discourse. However, some theologians like Isasi-Díaz reflect on this term and demonstrate an awareness of alternate Latino realities. The material for theology became *lo cotidiano*. This also highlighted the community's struggle for *sobrevivencia/supervivencia*. Isasi-Díaz turned to ethnography as a theological resource, and uncovered the need to include the other through *mulatez*. She also developed a *mujerista* theology that highlighted the plight of Hispanic women. She began to reveal more tensions present in *mestizaje* with her usage of *mulatez* and *mu-*

jerista theologies. Thus, there are more varied tensions within US Latino communities.

In this chapter we examined secular readings of *mestizaje* that are strong critiques of the term and made a return to a theological critique through Néstor Medina. Manuel Vásquez, an author that heavily critiqued *mestizaje* from a Central American context, argues that we must nuance our use of *mestizaje* because of the unfortunate history of the term in his context. He makes the case that theology must be aware of the other and proposes a tension of *mescolanza* and *otredad*. However, his use of *mescolanza* may be problematic. And while he encourages a transcultural *hibridez*, he does not discuss what this *hibridez* would look like.

Another author I have examined is Manuel De La Torre. He studied *mulatez* and reveals the history associated with this particular term. He states that *mulataje* cannot escape violence toward Africans. De La Torre reveals the importance to nuance our terminology, and for this reason we must discuss multiple realities. His usage is problematic in that he provides no alternate way of using the term in a positive dimension. Lastly, he provides no viable model for envisioning Hispanic/Latin@ communities in the US in light of his discussion.

The final author I have examined is Néstor Medina. He elucidates this discussion in that our terminology concerning *mestizaje* has two possible meanings: *mestizaje*-as mixture, or *mestizaje*-as miscegenation. After examining the discussion of *mestizaje*, Medina concludes that the Latino reality is a complex reality that is yet to be named, which is characterized by *mestizajes*.

I agree with Néstor Medina about the need to examine further the totality of peoples that compose the Hispanic community, and I think *mestizajes* is useful because it creates an awareness of divergent experiences in Latin America and consequently also in the US. He reveals the tension between a general reading of *mestizaje* and a specific reading of *mestizaje*. He revises this collapse by creating a general category of *mestizajes* to describe a comprehensive Latino identity.

Medina elucidates that there are variant experiences even within this community and we are not to stereotype them. This is important if we are to consider undocumented immigration. In any case, we must be careful with the terminology we employ because even though it has served as the *locus theologicus* of the Hispanic community it has been demonstrated by these authors and in Medina's discussion that there are problems with this term that may create epistemological violence on those who cannot claim it. For this reason, when we think of Latin America and Latinos in the US, we must build an intra-ethnic solidarity, as Vásquez has stated, and focus on a transcultural *hibridez* built upon a more nuanced understanding and discussion of *mestizaje*. We do not jettison the term *mestizaje* as it has revealed the nature of the community and it also points to its *cosmovisión(es)*. Rather we build upon it, recognizing that it has allowed us to examine our community and it will continue to be relevant to our community in future discourse. It is also a continuing identity marker for many communities in Latin America and in the US. However, though it has been the most dominant metanarrative it is not the overarching exclusive metanarrative for Latin America.

For instance, we must look at undocumented immigration, the story of the poor, marginalized, and oppressed, which history has taught us that they are mostly of Amerindian or African heritage. If we look at undocumented immigration, we are also to look at those who are outside the centers of power, being marginal par excellence. In trying to look at this perspective, it is necessary to look at the experience of marginalization. In order to do this, I propose the dialogue *identidad* and *otredad* present in *hibridez*.

One final point to stress is that *mestizaje* must make a return to theology at some point in time. It appears that some of its main concerns are sociological/anthropological. However, I want to ground *mestizaje* and *hibridez* solidly in theology. This shall come at a later point in this book through the Spirit of God's immanence and transcendence. For the time being, I shall continue discussing these cultural dimensions through *hibridez*. I shall run this thread through before I return to the theological task. Vásquez and De La Torre, for example, include almost no theological nuances. Medina makes a strong return to theology via *la Virgen de Guadalupe* in Roman Catholicism. I shall look at these and introduce a Pentecostal perspective on *hibridez* in later chapters. My goal is to observe the dynamics of *hibridez*, *identidad*, *otredad*, and *mestizaje* in God's nature. We must understand the multicultural reality as a profound liminal space that reflects God's relationship to the created order. I make this point in order to state that I have not forgotten this is a theological work. Again, I shall return to theology after a discussion on *hibridez*.

A study of *mestizaje* reveals that the Latino community is a complex reality that exists with a multiplicity of dimensions and tensions – I shall call these tensions *hibridez* and a movement between *identidad* and *otredad*. We have explored discussions on *mestizaje* and its implications for Latino *comsmovisiones*. One must be aware of and consider all dimensions of Latino life in the US – the tension and exchanges between *identidad* and *otredad*. The material for theological research expands including *mestizaje*, *mujerista* theology, and *mulatez*. It further expands also to include Amerindians, *zambedad*, and *indocumentados*.

5

HIBRIDEZ: THE EMERGENCE OF A WORLD TRAVELING HYBRIDITY

Introduction

We have explored *mestizaje* and have noticed that we must look more carefully at the Latino situation if we wish to describe or make sense of those who come from Latin America and those who dwell in the US. We are also to take a more nuanced look at these peoples if we are to build a theology of undocumented immigration from these countries. In what we have examined many authors are calling for the discussion to take a step back from its focus or readings on *mestizaje*, and observe the big picture to begin to consider what was suggested by Vásquez's *mescolanza* or by Medina's *mestizajes*. I suggest that the terminology we use to describe the people of Latin America must include the cultural, racial, and ethnic make-up of the people. I strongly suggest that it builds through a web of relationality further informed by hybridity as Vásquez has suggested. In this chapter I dialogue with a particular branch of learning that has contributed to hybridity: postcolonial theory. I do so in order to bring about a unique Latino understanding of *hibridez*.

In this chapter I offer a brief history of the term, *hibridez*. Later, I dialogue with hybridity to try to understand how this informs *hibridez*, *mestizajes*, or intermixture-*mestizaje*. I also point out that *hibridez* is not merely a translation of hybridity but points towards the unique experiences of Latinos. I also note that we have arrived at this juncture through *mestizaje*, and as such, it is grounded deeply in *lo cotidiano*. I am not merely inserting postcolonial hybridity into this book. Rather, I am dialoguing with it to compare and contrast with this discussion on *mestizaje*. I also wish to explore how a post-colonial hybridity may help an emerging Latino *hibridez*.

Divergence in *Hibridez*

The particular term, hybridity, has its own history that must be explored. The origin of this particular term is from the Latin, *hybrida*. It is a term borrowed from farming; its original usage referred to the offspring of a tamed sow and a wild boar. Later, it became a term to describe the children of a Roman citizen and a slave. Over time, it was employed by science to designate emerging varieties of plants.

In the 19th century, the terms, hybrid and hybridity, became physiological phenomena referring to miscegenation in the 19th century. Certain individuals were marked either as half-breeds or half-castes. Fixation on essentialism warned of possible dangers from any hybridization and also warned of possible degenerations that could result from the mixing of races that occupied different hierarchical positions in society. This anxiety about hybridity served to keep races separate.

Some caution us on the use of hybridity. First, it could collapse into an exclusive argument of biology.[1] This could derail a conversation on Latin American realities because it may collapse into a discussion on mere racial delineations. Like *mulatez* it may collapse into a negative reading because it points to a sterile animal, the mule. Another point against its usage is that it may connote a strict scientific determinism that does not necessarily capture Latin American *cosmovisiones*.[2] For example, if it is used in a strict scientific sense of scientific determinism as in the study of DNA and varieties resulting from intermixture it could potentially collapse into a closed scientific worldview that rejects spiritual and preternatural possibilities. Such is a position that contradicts Latino *cosmovisiones* and those of Amerindians and other groups such as Africans in the Americas.

---

[1] Néstor García Canclini, 'Culturas Híbridas y estrategias comunicacionales', *Estudios sobre las culturas contemporaneas* 3.5 (June 1997), pp. 109-28 (p. 110).

[2] Néstor García Canclini, *Hybrid Cultures: Strategies for Entering and Leaving Modernity* (Minneapolis: University of Minnesota Press, 1995), p. 265.

However, I propose that it if we use the Latin root *hybrida* and connect it to *mestizaje* and *lo cotidiano*, the resulting *hibridez* is a term that may be redeemed for theological use because it is a term that points to a place of creativity, creation, and ethnogenesis. For example, it points to interdisciplinary creativity where forms and meanings are negotiated.[3] It may also help move stagnant dialogue forward in order to expose intra-hispanic dynamics and those towards the outside of the Hispanic community. For example, Honduran-Americans negotiate their identity in slightly different ways than Mexican–Americans or Puerto Ricans. There are vivid exchanges where one word is offensive to one nationality but not to another. For example, Hondurans use the term *vos* to address people. It indicates familiarity, closeness, and friendship. However, used in the wrong context it can be offensive to someone. Other parts of Latin America, such as Puerto Rico or Mexico, do not readily use *vos*. They prefer *tú*. Without knowing it, a Honduran could offend a fellow Latin American.

I also think it helps us understand Latino relations to those outside the Latino community, such as African-Americans in the urban enclaves such as Harlem. Such dialogues between different Latino communities in the US towards the outside of these communities help us to *matizar* (nuance) different currents in dialogue.[4] For example, I think it may help us explain the case of second, third, fourth, etc., generation Latinos in the US who find more of an affinity with US mainstream culture than with those who come from Latin America. For example, in the church I pastored in New York City, the children preferred fast food burgers over *baleadas* or *pupusas*.

I also note that I am not merely translating the term hybridity and merely using the Spanish form of the term. I appeal to the original Latin use of *hybrida* and the connection to the Latin roots of Spanish. The Spanish term, *híbrido*, and its derivative, *hibridez*, may aid us to recover the particular experiences of Latino communities that Elizondo evoked through *mestizaje*, but it must always re-

---

[3] Prabhu, *Hybridity*, p. xi.

[4] Chiara Donadoni and Eugenia Houvenaghel, 'La Hibridez de la tradición judeocristiana como reivinidicación del sincretismo religioso de la nueva España: El divino narciso de Sor Juana', *Neophilologus* 94 (2010), pp. 459-75 (p. 474).

main open to dialogue from within Latino communities. I also think that it is a term that may lead to dialogue with those outside Latino communities, such as immigrants from Africa, Asia, and Europe to the US. Case in point, I once met a young Guatemalan woman that was of direct Chinese ancestry in Manhattan. She spoke fluent Spanish and no Chinese. She claimed to be Guatemalan.

Through *lo cotidiano*, we are able to observe complex layers of *hibridez*. This complexity includes the tension of *identidad* and *otredad* as currents that shape the Latino experience, especially when immigrating to the US and as second and third generations adapt to life in the US. These are in dialogue through *encuentros, encontronazos, reencuentros* and *desencuentros*. These in turn shape this *hibridez*. *Hibridez* helps us understand the decentering of the totalizing universal self or of totalitarian tendencies, and reveals a continual process of hospitality.

In the case of Honduras, many experience the *otredad* of not being *mestizo* or not even *mulato*, demonstrating the recurring Latin American critique of *mestizaje*. Some experience the *otredad* of not being able to survive in their context and thus opt for the experience of migration to the US and other nations. Through the usage of *hibridez*, I am trying to nuance *mestizaje* to serve the purpose of doing theology from an undocumented perspective so that its principles and ideas may include groups that may not be necessarily included within *metizaje*'s scope and that we may resist totalizing tendencies.

My understanding of *hibridez* speaks from the reality of Latin America and from undocumented immigration. For this reason, *hibridez* must also remain grounded in *lo cotidiano*, otherwise it falls apart into meta-theorizing and intellectual discourse without praxis. Thus, *hibridez* remains tightly connected to *mestizaje* and cannot exist apart from it. This has been one of the strongest critiques of postcolonial hybridity. Many see it as a concept of the elite or only for the privileged.[5] It is also critiqued as using a highly convoluted discourse that obstructs the reality of a violent colonial past and its ongoing repercussions.[6] As I dialogue with its discourse I wish to

---

[5] Prabhu, *Hybridity*, p. 12.

[6] Jane Hiddleston, *Understanding Movements in Modern Thought: Understanding Postcolonialism* (Durham: Acumen, 2009), p. 121.

make it clear that I maintain a bridge to Medina's *mestizajes*, this understanding of *hibridez* strives to remain grounded in *lo cotidiano* and therefore build bridges to Latino realities of *supervivencia* – which includes undocumented immigration.

Hibridez and Homi K. Bhabha's Hybridity

Homi K. Bhabha is one of the most easily recognized figures that speaks of postcolonial hybridity. He was born in Mumbai to the minority Parsi community. He later studied in Oxford and taught in Sussex and Chicago. He currently teaches at Harvard. He is particularly sensitive to hybridity as discrepant cultural meanings produced by heterogeneous people of a nation in interpreting and reinterpreting the dominant culture. Bhabha is far removed from the Latin American or US Hispanic reality. But his ideas on hybridity have been put to use in an examination of the consequences and fallout resulting from colonial and postcolonial encounters.

There must be more dialogue between differing multicultural realities. If there are hybrid<u>ities</u> (underline mine) or *variedades*, these must dialogue with each other. The reason for continued dialogue with Bhabha is that in the case of Honduras there has been a *coloso al Norte* that has dictated world policy and its stance is similar to a power dictating the way things should be economically, culturally, and politically. Furthermore, Latinos in the US always negotiate and navigate their position with mainstream culture.

I emphasize this also: I purposefully engage these different realities much in the way hybridity occurs: engaging two apparently discrepant realities in order to arise with new meanings and life for these realities. I examine some of Bhabha's main elements in his theory on hybridity and will later give positives and negatives and possible synthetic elements that may be compatible with *mestizaje* and *lo cotidiano*. I further propose that while they are similar, hybridity and *hibridez* are also different.

Bhabha redeems the terms hybrid and hybridity by acknowledging their history. He notes that in his context in India it served to reinforce racial and cultural separation by creating anxiety about mixtures. However, this same time period experienced disturbances in the general order of colonial societies. Encounters between colonizer and native did not always remain neatly apart or separately defined.

Babha states that an ahistorical 19[7] century polarity of East and West created exclusionary imperialist ideologies of the self and other.[7] However, during this same time, there was also an inevitable mixing in the colonies extending to all areas of colonial life. These interactins created ruptures and tensions that were far more complex than easy categories imposed by the colonial system. Those in his native lands adapted Western customs and appropriated them with their own meaning.

The specific biological mixture of East and West forced a re-thinking of inscriptions in laws and policies that managed and over-saw colonial activities. For example, the question of mixture required the colonists to engage with the mixed section of the population when it came to inheritance, education, burials, marriage, and the notion of citizenship.[8] Consequently, they also faced intellectual and cultural mixtures that called into question the neat division between the two groups. These became questions that dealt with customs and traditions. Such tensions affected several dimensions of identity and revealed tensions in interactions between the subaltern and dominant cultures in all areas of life.

Liminal Space, Interstitial Category

For Bhabha, hybridity is a liminal or interstitial category in identity that occupies a space between competing or coexisting cultural traditions, historical periods, and critical methodologies.[9] Many colonial subjects found themselves in this liminal space in a state of resistance against imperial oppression. In the case of the Two-Thirds World (a term I prefer over less developed countries) they were playing catch-up to affluent Western societies economically, technologically, and developmentally.

For Bhabha the colonized form a passive resistance through hybrid mimicry. This mimicry is a repetition of the already existing narratives while simultaneously subverting them. This means that the colonial power's effect is to produce hybridization rather than its ultimate goal of full assimilation. The colonial power also fails to

---

[7] Bhabha, *The Location of Culture*, p. 37.
[8] Prabhu, *Hybridity*, p. xi.
[9] Bhabha, *The Location of Culture*, p. 107.

repress these hybrid expressions. Interactions of the oppressed with dominant traditions create a dissonance with existing norms and alternate perspectives.[10] This is not done arbitrarily but negotiated across differences of nations, community interests, and cultural values.[11] It eventually leads to a reformulation or a critique of the colonial authority in light of nuanced understandings of the colonizer's power. It also leads to the formation of heteroglossia as the marginalized create expressions that produce two simultaneous meanings or that express two different viewpoints simultaneously.[12]

Bhabha's understanding of hybridity demonstrates cultural identities are complex and create increasing complexity for created categories such as ethnicity and race. While hybridity may refer to physiological changes and intermixture it goes beyond these and examines intellectual, cultural, and philosophical interchanges. It is by going beyond physiological factors that hybridity reveals and provides recognition for and legitimizes the subaltern constituencies.[13] In other words, those on the margins may be understood on their own terms. Simultaneously, they make meaning of hidden things that speaks directly or indirectly about existence on the margins.

Bhabha highlights this change of meaning and legitimizes them. Moreover, he describes continual exchanges in this hybridity. Meanings of forms and narratives are constantly negotiated. Hybridity is not just the reproduction or regurgitation of meaning; rather, it is an in-between space that produces diverse meanings, and more heteroglossic expression.[14] It is a type of cultural engagement and exchanges may produce two polarities in a broad spectrum either antagonistic or affiliative to the colonizer or colonized. The differences emerge performatively or in the act of re-presentation of these ideas. In other words, while lacking a written expression, they may emerge by the actions of a community or people. One of these actions is immigration. It produces exchanges yielding complex cul-

---

[10] Bhabha, *The Location of Culture*, p. 112.

[11] Bhabha, *The Location of Culture*, p. 2.

[12] Marisol de la Cadena, '¿Son Mestizos los Híbridos? Las Políticas Conceptuales de las Identidades Andinas', *Unversitas Humanística* 61 (enero-junio 2006), pp. 51-84 (p. 51).

[13] Prabhu, *Hybridity*, p. xi.

[14] De La Cadena, '¿Son Mestizos los Híbridos? Las Políticas Conceptuales de las Identidades Andinas', p. 51.

tural identities in which one may not fit in preconceived molds anymore. The colonized is involved in a complex on-going negotiation that seeks to authorize and validate cultural hybridities.[15]

These tensions consequently have important consequences for analyzing the other. The other gains strength through a political and, what Bhabha calls, an agnostic process.[16] Bhabha states: 'dissensus, alterity and otherness are the discursive conditions for the circulation and recognition of a politicized subject and a public truth'.[17] It becomes primordial to recognize the historical and discursive otherness.[18]

A vision of otherness places the focus of his study on the phenomenological outcome of the cultural interpretations and reinterpretations of colonial authority. We continue to build bridges to *lo cotidiano* as a source for reflection. In this movement, one gains a sense of a dialectical movement between the self and the other that results in a variety of expressions. The colonized synthesize modalities and there is no such thing as full assimilation. Bhabha uses the metaphor of a bridge being the interstitial space that unites two different riverbanks – both the colonizer and the colonized. The bridge is a place of traffic where people cross and stop at different rates. Some dialogue, some collide, some don't acknowledge the other, while some are permanently on the bridge. An emerging notion of *hibridez* calls us to affirm racial mixing, and also to be on the bridge to be active participants of *encuentros* and to participate purposefully in dialogue.

Hibridez makes us aware of forms of resistance to dynamics of identity and forms of appropriation of these dynamics. In the case of undocumented immigration there are legitimate reasons these people make their journey *al norte*. These dynamics must be understood in order to establish a place from which to begin theological reflection.

Qualifying an Emerging *Hibridez*

The Latino context can be very diverse, especially in urban jungles. In the case of immigration, those outside the centers of power

---

[15] Bhabha, *The Location of Culture*, p. 2.
[16] Bhabha, *The Location of Culture*, p. 37.
[17] Bhabha, *The Location of Culture*, p. 37.
[18] Bhabha, *The Location of Culture*, p. 38.

adapt to the new cultural center and interact with it freely. Those on the margins respond to the new traditions with innovation. They are free to be subversive to their surrounding oppression even in passive ways. In many ways, *hibridez* calls a Latino identity to this liminal or interstitial space towards a meaningful or purposeful dialogue between *identidad* and *otredad* producing *encuentros, reencuentros,* and *desencuentros.*

One major difference with Bhabha is that we may question just how free the people in Latin America are to interact with the centers of power. The problem of violence in Latin America has had a presence that continues to limit the freedom of the people involved. Whether military states, or abuse by the police or armed forces, to criminality and drug cartels, and impunity, violence is one dimension that marks Latin America and creates questions about the relative freedom of individuals and communities to interact freely with those in power. Even ecclesiologically, it may be questionable how free they have been to interact with paternalistic models of mission or establish their own leadership.

It is important to understand the nature of the interaction with US mainstream culture and other cultures in the US as Latinos deal with different interactions on a daily basis. This is another way *hibridez* may connect with Bhabha's hybridity. US neoliberal capitalism and the technological dissemination of information are powerful forces to which many are continually adapting. In many ways there are several different reactions or engagements and entanglements with the influence of the US in Latin America. Reactions across the spectrum point to stiff opposition like that of Chavismo in Venezuela or close cooperation like countries such as Honduras where the US has a continued military presence in the Palmerola base in Comayagua. In practice there is a continuing struggle coming to terms with the realities produced by this *encuentro* with this colossal power.

Hibridez points to a place or a reality where such disparate realities converge. These *encuentros* are between *identidad* and *otredad.* It is a liminal place where we see the negotiation of identity in which a person identifies with the two distinct realities. This identification may produce a multiple embeddedness in two cultures, or that of being a bridge person. This multiple embeddedness may be both positive and negative. It is negative in the sense that it diffuses identity so that one is neither-nor a part of this or that group. It creates a squall in which one does not belong to either world. However, it is also positive in the sense that it affirms an in-between identity. A bridge person is also able to speak on both riverbanks and to the inhabitants of both sides. Such is the case of many Latinos that prefer burgers to tacos, fast food over *mondongo*, and who have found their home in mainstream US culture.

A difference between *hibridez* and Bhabha's intellectual discourse on *hybridity* is that it cannot become highly convoluted discourse. There must be a lot of caution in using his works because it may become a highly ethereal discourse without touching the reality of *lo cotidiano*. For example, the US always raises the question of race to the forefront, as mere appearances are enough to make people judge another. We must never stop making room for those who do not fit in Black versus White categories.

Nonetheless, Bhabha pushes us towards philosophical and cultural negotiation by demonstrating how a liminal space is also a creative place of innovation and this creative energy may inform an emerging *hibridez*. The dialogue between *identidad* and *otredad* takes place here. In our discussion on *mestizaje* we incorporate the other into the discussion and begin to explore theological approaches to the question of the other, like *mulato*, *zambo*, and Amerindian identities. It also provides a tool to understand the dynamics between these groups. *Hibridez* takes us into the threshold where *identidad* and *otredad* meet.

There is also the caution of asking just how free these people are in their agency in *hibridez*. It appears that many times in Latin America freedom is enacted in the form of passive resistance. Undocumented immigration is a form of passive resistance. Individuals and communities move *al norte* quietly through cracks on the border and hide in urban ghettos while working in jobs no one else seems to want to do. This is but one reality surfacing from *lo cotidiano* and informing the discourse on *hibridez*. *Hibridez* must recognize modifications and divergent heteroglossic voices arising from the Latino community. It must also seek to be a bridge uniting two opposing forces of dialogue or conflict.

Hibridez y Globalización

Globalization and global capitalism impose a form of colonialism on the rest of the world. I want to suggest that from a Latino perspective one such form of resistance is undocumented immigration. It is a phenomenological form of resistance and a way to cope with suffocating experiences of poverty in the two-thirds world. Immigration is a way of improvisation for the poor masses. The poor know all about the riches of Europe and North America for they are saturated with its media and receive information from them through technology. Ubiquitous computing through mobile devices, the Information Age, and the propagation of the Internet make such information readily available in many countries. They consume these realities that they may not be able to participate in. Thus they are on the fences looking in.

For the sake of clarity, I give a more vivid example: I went to a North American fast food restaurant in Tegucigalpa. As I sat down to eat, I felt such *vergüenza* as barefoot children in dirty tattered clothes pressed their faces on the clean crystal and asked for a bite to eat. A security guard clad in military-like uniform guarded the entrance to the restaurant with an automatic machine gun. The contrast was disturbing – nauseating really. What do these poor children do? How do they cope or how do they become actors upon their reality? They turn to violence, crime, or immigrate. The child refugee crisis is one expression of this reality. They came fleeing hopeless situations only to find North Americans with closed minds and closed doors rejecting them. Meanwhile, the Church kept silent.

The outsourcing of labor from the US to poorer nations also has consequences in these countries. Foreign companies invest in manual labor such as the *maquilas* in northern Honduras and *camaroneras* in southern Honduras, but these exchanges are seldom unilateral processes. Neither do they stay in tidy neat categories. Such outsourcing has messy consequences. For example, the work goes overseas, but the laborers are expected to stay put.[19] It is not this simple. This outsourcing creates tumultuous circumstances and global competition creates tempestuous and uncertain positions for

---

[19] Orlando Espín, 'Immigration, Territory, and Globalization: Theological Reflections', *Journal of Hispanic Latino Theology* 10 (Fall 2006), pp. 46-59 (pp. 52-53).

the working poor. A transnational company may easily pick up and leave to another country where labor costs less.

Immigration cannot be naïvely viewed today as the movement of individuals or groups from one geographic location to another, nor as the crossing of national boundaries.[20] People migrate because they want to find employment in order to feed their families, relieve their hunger, educate their children, have some sort of health care, and be able to retire during their golden years.[21] Immigrants want work, not handouts.

In this same way we realize that borders exist, but less and less as barriers. Borders are increasingly porous and often de-territorialized. Migration brings people together. Orlando Espín believes that in light of such circumstances we need an ecclesiology that takes seriously the issues raised by immigration and construct an entire ecclesiological construct from the perspective of immigration.[22]

Heteroglossic Visions in *Hibridez*

An example of *heteroglossic* interpretation by the immigrants of the US is *el Sueño Americano*. This has interesting connotations in the Spanish. When referring to what most Americans call America they use the term, *Estados Unidos*. An American is an *Estadounidense*. When referring to themselves even in their home countries, they know themselves as *Americanos* because they are taught that they too live in America, as in the American continent. Thus, the American dream is also their dream because they are Americans, as in Latin American or from the American continent.

One of the ways to participate in such society is *a la brava* or by force without consideration and without circumspection about minor consequences such as a fine or the threat of deportation. On account of their starving children, failed crops, and employment the present becomes a time of action. They travel through crime ridden areas, assaulted, raped, maimed by the infamous train called, *la Bestia*, and move through deserts enduring hunger and thirst because they are enduring one of the worst forms of initiation into the North American Dream. In the meantime, connections to commu-

---

[20] Espín, 'Immigration, Territory, and Globalization', p. 53.
[21] Espín, 'Immigration, Territory, and Globalization', p. 53
[22] Espín, 'Immigration, Territory, and Globalization', p. 54.

nity and family give them hope because they know people who have been successful *en el norte*. They have heard and seen that there is a way, and that way is *al norte*. They walk through deserts in order to *lograr el sueño Americano*, a dream that they know is within their reach.

Away from Racial Delineations

Another area that we can build to connect here is a movement away from the original entanglement of this idea with the notion of race. For example, being Latino does not mean being part of a particular race. Nonetheless, this concerns many Latinos because a vast majority of them are non-white. In the context of the US, Latinos include many Amerindian immigrants whose roots have been truncated by colonial experience.

Many people from Mexico, for example, are of indigenous heritage. They are marginalized by social structures, even by other Latinos. It is common to walk down a predominantly Mexican neighborhood in the US and hear their languages, like Mizteco, Zapoteco, and Chinanteco. In New York, where I pastored, some learned Spanish until they crossed the border and started living in the US. Such discoveries reveal the reality of the suffering poor, indigenous, and marginalized, whose way of hope is through the experience of immigration.

Cosmovisiones

Hibridez is also present in their appropriation of symbols of their faith such as saints and *la Virgen de Guadalupe* as belonging to their *cosmovisión*.[23] Thus, we must locate them and understand them in light of their historical circumstances. We are to understand the nuances in their identity especially since Jorge J.E. Gracia describes their identity as not tied down to race or ethnicity but as existing in a web of relationships.[24] We continue to build bridges to their religious expressions because this reveals a lot about their *cosmovisión* and ultimately their *identidad*. Gracia states that membership in the

---

[23] Daniel Ramírez, 'Call Me "Bitter": Life and Death in the Diasporic Borderland and the Challenges/Opportunities for Norteamericano Churches', *Perspectivas* 11 (Fall 2007), p. 40.

[24] Jorge J.E. Gracia, 'Ethnic Labels and Philosophy: the Case of Latin American Philosophy', in Eduardo Mendieta (ed.), *Latin American Philosophy, Currents, Issues, Debates* (Bloomington, IN: Indiana University Press, 2003), pp. 57-67 (p. 58).

category of Hispanic or Latino is not a matter of apodictic certainty.[25] Rather, in Latin America, it is more or less, and not necessarily a yes or no. Consequently, it is a matter of ontological reality consisting of a web of relations to many other things.[26] Just because one speaks Spanish does not make him or her Latino. Many second-generation immigrants do not speak Spanish at home.

I state this because the nature of being Latino is a complex proposition. It is the result of many influences, such as colonial, Amerindian, African, etc. This complex web of relations forms this identity and is not limited exclusively to race. There are intersections of multiplicity, plurality, and difference in less specifiable ways. These are very relevant in a discussion of *cosmovisión* because those who enter the US engage in the work of improvisation, learning, adapting, and adjusting.

A common colonial thread may connect Latinos but there are expressions and experiences diverse regionally, internationally, and intra-nationally. For example, in the case of Latinos some are *mestizo* or *mulato*, and some are not. Some may be Honduran, Bolivian, Uruguayan, Puerto Rican, or Mexican. Even in Honduras, some may be *mestizo*, *zambo*, or Amerindian such as the Pech, *Tolupán*, Lenca, *Miskito*, or *Garífuna*. Thus we may include several factors in Latin America that have to do with immigration *al norte*. One must enter the lives of the poor and their movements. These are most likely to initiate movements across physical and national borders. The interactions between different Latino groups is a form of *hibridez* and should be studied further.

Violencia

If we incorporate *lo cotidiano* in this *hibridez*, we must also include discussions on the violence of Latin America and the victims of violence.[27] In 2012, Honduras had the highest murder rate in the world at nearly three times the international average and nearly

---

[25] Gracia, 'Ethnic Labels and Philosophy', p. 65.

[26] Gracia, 'Ethnic Labels and Philosophy', p. 65.

[27] Diario La Prensa, 'María Otero: Ponerle fin a al impunidad es clave', *La Prensa*, http://www.laprensa.hn/Secciones-Principales/Honduras/Tegucigalpa/Maria-Otero-Ponerle-fin-a-la-impunidad-es-clave#.UFdIX0LffEU (accessed Sept. 14, 2012).

twenty times that of the US.[28] Drug trafficking was at an all-time high.[29] People helped drug smugglers because they paid a higher wage than the transnational companies who outsource labor to their countries. Drug smuggling also gave employment opportunities in impoverished areas where no transnational company dared to go, or where jobs had been sent to another part of the world where labor costs less. There has also developed a culture of *maras* and *pandillas* that contribute to crime and violence. The corruption of the police and the corruption of the government in Honduras made it difficult because the police easily accepted bribes. There was a scandal in 2011 where it was discovered that the police participated in violent crimes, ran drug trafficking rings, and were members of violent gangs. In the case of Honduras, there has been a fear of destabilization because of such violence, impunity, and the participation of authorities in criminal activity.

Consequently, many of those under the grip of violence, insecurity, and poverty choose a way out. Many have chosen the relative peace of their neighbor *al norte*. For the work in undocumented immigration, it means recognizing the radical disparity of those south of the US-Mexico border, and the historical conditions that have caused a mass exodus of people. This is the Honduran version of diasporization, a forced *irrupción* into the US.

Agency

If we are to continue looking at otherness and the other, we must recapture the notion of agency. We are always challenged by the stunning inequality of two groups of people locked into a relationship of domination that is upheld and perpetuated by a system that operates in the sphere of the psychological and symbolic as much as in the economic and structural.[30] Such is the case of undocumented persons. They are at the mercy of a voting constituency

---

[28] Diario La Prensa, 'La Violencia ha dejado 46,450 muertos en Honduras en los Últimos Once Años', *La Prensa*, http://www.elheraldo.hn/Secciones-Princip ales/Al-Frente/La-violencia-ha-dejado-46-450-muertos-en-Honduras-en-los-ulti mos-once-anos (accessed March 12, 2012).

[29] Diario La Prensa, 'Honduras Continúa en la Lista Negra de EUA en Tránsito Ilícito de Droga', *La Prensa*, http://www.laprensa.hn/Secciones-Princip ales/Honduras/Tegucigalpa/Honduras-continua-en-lista-negra-de-EUA-en-trans ito-de-drogas-ilicitas#.UFdHskLffEU (accessed Sept. 14, 2012).

[30] Prabhu, *Hybridity*, p. xiv.

that seems to scapegoat them for the nation's economic ills. Furthermore, Politicians seeking votes – both Democrat *and* Republican in the US – unashamedly throw them around and stereotype them in order to get a vote. Consequently, a discussion of the other in *hibridez* challenges us to establish nonhierarchical connections and to encourage lateral relations. The hope of postcolonial theorist, Prabhu, is that instead of living within the bounds created by a linear view of history and society, we become free to interact on an equal footing with all the traditions that determine our present predicament.[31] So we come to a place where we create room to recognize the legitimate personality and cultural traditions of the marginalized subject, despite the dissimilarity, contrast, disparity, or variation to that of the center of power. We recognize, validate, and legitimize the racial make-up, historical roots, and cultural traditions of that subject.

If *hibridez* is a dimension that can be applied to Latino peoples in the US, we are seeing an alternate community with variant yet legitimate understandings of what it means to be American. We must acknowledge the great sociocultural, ethnic, racial, and class differences in Latin America that have produced a great influx from Latin America to the US. These will produce different understandings of the American Dream and will cope with liberal democracy in different ways. Undocumented immigration is a small yet significant expression of such interpretation. As such, it has produced other ways for becoming or being an American. We must also be aware of children who go to school their whole lives in the American system only to be denied the opportunity for further education or self-improvement because their parents brought them here when they were but infants or toddlers. They say the pledge of allegiance every day but are never given the opportunity to live it out. We must also recognize families forcefully broken up by absurd immigration policy.

Liminal Space

Hibridity also means that there may be a condition of being halfway, between, and not defined. Bhbaha argues that interpretations move somewhere beyond control but not beyond accommodation.[32] Some-

---

[31] Prabhu, *Hybridity*, p. 6.
[32] Bhabha, *The Location of Culture*, p. 18.

times, this type of existence can lead to a double self, or a fragmented identity. However, it can also be a place where people become bridge people being able to connect two opposing cultural
groups. So there is a sense of having a diffused identity or of embracing that identity as a bridge person.

In the case of many Latinos, they experience a sense of belonging to both sides of the American border. What many US citizens
fail to realize is that their forefathers and their history is strikingly
similar. Many Europeans arrived in this country with little or minute
knowledge of the English language or mainstream American culture and with little or no possessions in order to start their lives
anew. Ellis Island in New York Harbor is a vivid reminder of this
reality. One can go into the museum and look at artifacts from the
late 19th century and early 20th century. One can also see the lack of
schooling that people had and the poverty that they were seeking to
escape. There are also Nativist restrictions imposed on those who
came to the US looking for a new way of life.

The people of Latin America have had similar experiences and
are bound by historical experiences to their North American peers.
Nonetheless, they are moving in a new context and creating new
spaces with the great variety they bring with them. *Hibridez* means
we create space for a general sense of being American, a general
sense for being Latino, but there is also room for specific ways of
being Latino or Latin American. *Hibridez* takes us towards this intentional world traveling and sensitivity to the other.

Hybridity and *Hibridez*

Hybridity is a complex notion that may inform the development of
a Latin American *hibridez*. We have seen that the way we engage the
other is one of the most primordial concerns. I have built bridges
from a Latino vantage point and describe similar occurrences in
Latin America and the US. However, I maintain that these have experiences that differ from Bhabha's context. I differentiate between
the terms hybridity and *hibridez*. In understanding this contrast,
hibridez may allow us to enter the conversation and engage the interrelationship of the self and other through a distinct experience that
mestizaje revealed through *lo cotidiano*. An ethic of *hibridez* demands
hospitality towards the other. I also examined how this interchange

plays out in regards to the case of some Latinos in the US. A dialogue between *mestizaje* and *hibridez* allows us to carve out space for those that do not fit neatly in our categories including undocumented immigrants.

Hibridez also allows disparate entities to converge and dialogue. Also, it allows us to talk of Latino communities in a US in a general sense. It creates a commonality to an experience of diasporization and hybridization of those who enter the US. It also points to neo-colonial factors created by global capitalism that create the issue of undocumented immigration. As such, it must be considered an important factor in the identity of the Latino community in the US, including undocumented immigrants from Latin America.

Hibridez needs to be tempered by the specific experience of Latin America and of US Hispanics towards which *mestizaje* points. For example, Bhabha points to useful metaphors and tools we can use, such as heteroglossic voice and that of being bridge people. However, his context and his discourse are not compatible with Latin America. *Hibridez* is thus similar and dissimilar to *hybridity*. Most importantly, I repeat this in order to get the point across strongly: *hibridez* must be grounded in *lo cotidiano*, otherwise *hibridez* becomes a highly convoluted discourse with no participation in the lives of the poor and marginalized. *Hibridez* serves as a complement to the discussion of *mestizaje* or as an ever-present qualifier to understand the condition of *mestizaje* and other Latino and Latin American conditions. It also allows us to take a step back and look at the *variedades* of experiences in Latin America and it demonstrates this diversity. This diversity allows us to think in terms of inter-human relationships and of identity in terms of a web of relationality with degrees of relationality, and a multiple embeddedness that accompanies such experiences. These are concepts that help our discussion on *mestizaje* and help to sensitize our discussion to the plight of undocumented immigrants in the US. *Hibridez* is also useful to try to come to terms with the economic dominance of the US and the push-pull factors that go into immigration. These are concepts for future dialogue and adaptation.

These matters move theology towards a posture of dialogue and mutuality. *Hibridez* leads us to examine principles of *mestizaje*-intermixture, ultimately revealing tensions between the self and the other, or *identidad* and *otredad*. *Hibridez* is the experience and movement between *identidad* and *otredad*. Depending on the experience it may be a delicate dance or a tumultuous back-and-forth experience similar to the incessant motion of pistons in a car engine.

The experiences of *hibridez* are called *encuentros, reencuentros, encontronazos,* and *desencuentros.* In what follows I propose some terms that may help us understand the dynamics between *identidad* and *otredad* and the relationships resulting from *encuentros* between these that qualify an emerging *hibridez.* These exist in tension with each other and are always interacting, moving towards each other or away from each other. *Hibridez* relates to more than the racial mixing that characterizes Latin American peoples, it is the mixture of *cosmovisiones.*

Identidad, Otredad, and Encuentros

So in light of the previous discussion I will now try to describe the terms present in *hibridez.* I use my own language in order to begin to build a theology of encounter. *Identidad* refers to the self and to the construct known as the self or the social self. It is a product of social location and a cultural construct. It is a conjunction of shared characteristics of an individual and a collective whole. These characteristics are compared over against the other in their midst. It is also a consciousness often aware of being distinct and different or separate from the other.

Otredad refers to otherness. It may be a distinction performed by *identidad* or a distinction from *identidad.* *Otredad* is perceived as incongruous, incompatible, or out of place. *Otredad* may be a competitor or rejected. However, *otredad* also presents an opportunity for dialogue and for mutuality and just relationships.

These interactions between *identidad* and *otredad* are called *encuentros.* An *encuentro* can be positive or abrasive. It may foster a sense of mutuality or create a sense of antagonism or angst. *Encuentro* is a term that has been used by Latino Theologians for theological meetings and may represent places of dialogue in order to build understanding. Such usage can put positive connotations on the usage of this term. But an *encuentro* refers to an experience. Latinos remember their experiences and the nature of their relationship with individuals. It is in this experience that *identidad* and *otredad* meet. It is the experience that creates memories of the other and sets up possible future interactions. It is not merely an intellectual exercise but refers to the process of interaction as a whole. Tastes, sounds, smells, as well as ideas are all put into play in an *encuentro*.

Reencuentros are continued interactions. It may be a date set in the future. Also, once there it may also be a return to the past. It is also a way to build bridges forward. It speaks of a continued relationship and continual dialogue. Ideally, it speaks to the notion of the need of *amistad*, *hermandad*, and *fraternidad* that must qualify the process of *hibridez*.

Encontronazos refer to messy interactions. Its closest translation to English is a collision. It may refer to a stiff blow. It also refers to a sense of unraveling and destruction *encuentros* may produce which can do a number of things for theological dialogue. An *encontronazo* may produce harm so that it hurts one party or both. However, it may be a positive opportunity to awaken someone. It may also signal a change of direction or it may create more conflict. Generally, *encontronazos* do not have enough time for reflection and much like a boat leave a wake behind them. Similar to what is left behind in a collision one must gather the pieces after a crash or make sense of the *encontronazo*. Sometimes the blows are intentional and there are victims. Sometimes the blows are accidental and there are misunderstandings. Inevitably there must be a process of dialogue post-*encontronazo* for healing to occur and to gain a sense of mutuality. The most powerful *encontronazo* for Latinos came in 1492 when Columbus set foot in America.

Desencuentro refers to disagreement and discord. This is the result of a lack of understanding, unmet expectations, purposeful offense, or an unwillingness to change. It is a missed opportunity during an *encuentro*. Willingness is the key for dialogue and those that do not show this or resist it risk losing an opportunity for mutuality in a *desencuentro*. It refers to the negative experience of *encuentros*. However, one may never completely assimilate another's thought or personhood, so there is a sense that there must be a healthy distance or space with the other.

My goal in using these terms is to emphasize relationship and the affective move to *desire* to build just relationships. Through reflection on these experiences, we can begin to nuance Latin American situations and describe the fallout starting with the *encuentros* the first Amerindians experienced in the land they settled including the *encontronazo* of 1492. Many authors believe Latin America still bleeds from the consequence of this event.[33] Hence we are moved to *encuentros* and *reencuentros* of confession that move towards healing.

The values that must enter into *hibridez* are those of *fraternidad*, *hermandad*, and *amistad*. This is accomplished in a return to theology when the Holy Spirit decenters the self and moves us away from our drives of totalization towards hospitality towards the other. Finally, *hibridez* must continue to engage *mestizaje* because it gives *hibridez* a necessary historical grounding. *Hibridez* leads us to consider *otredad* and *identidad* within *mestizaje*. It also leads us to consider *identidad* and *otredad* outside of *mestizaje* such as mainstream US culture, *mulatez*, Amerindian realities, Caucasians, African Americans, undocumented immigrants, and vice versa. It allows us to nuance the *encuentros*, *reencuentros*, *encontronazos*, and *desencuentros* of the people of Latin America or those in the US through a dialogue between *identidad* and *otredad*. *Hibridez* becomes an identity marker as well as a methodology for an intercultural dialogue. This is what I think Medina hinted at through *mestizajes* and *mestizaje*-intermixture.

There are three directions *hibridez* takes us. First, it allows us to glimpse a web of relationality that constitutes Latino communities and the diversity therein. Second, it also allows us to move to interactions beyond the community to other realities outside US Latino communities. Third, it also allows us to describe these processes by describing the nuances in the web of relationality.

I strongly reemphasize that if we embrace and use *hibridez* we must remain grounded in *lo cotidiano* and *mestizaje*. We cannot escape the reality of the suffering people of Latin America or the visceral reality of the working urban poor in the US. *Lo cotidiano* is also necessary to build an authentic Latino theology. It allows us to include the poor in our theology. Furthermore, *hibridez* must not collapse into a rigidly closed scientific system with an equally closed and rigid scientific worldview. The *cosmovisiones* of Latin America do not allow for this. For this reason, we must allow for a dimension informed by God's immanent and transcendent Spirit active in *lo cotidiano* if we are to make use of *hibridez*. It is through this inclusion of God's Spirit in *lo cotidiano* that I make a return to theology

---

[33] Alma Guillermoprieto, *The Heart that Bleeds: Latin America Now* (New York: First Vintage Books, 1995), p. xiii.

through *hibridez*. The Spirit is active in the liminal space, actively calling us to hospitality.

Hibridez leads us to the metaphor of bridges as a place of exchanges. These bridges allow for a variety of responses and nuances to assimilation and appropriation of ideas and the re-presentation of these. We have *identidad* on one side of this bridge with *otredad* on the other. The traffic on the bridge negotiates *encuentros* between them. For example, a person that knows no English coming to the US and trying to live here experiences all kinds of *encontronazos*. More specifically an undocumented worker experiences all sorts of pressures and tensions from the society around them, first with the one they leave and second with the new one they enter. Such struggles include power relations such as when they are employed by people who turn a blind eye to the fact that they have no proper documentation and who also pay them below minimal wage for long hours of work.

Hibridez builds bridges within the Latino community and towards the outside of this community. It helps us understand *indocumentados* who make the journey *al norte*. We open up more dimensions arising from *lo cotidiano* that open up to *re-presentaciones híbridas*, such as *el Sueño Americano*, or the many issues people from Latin America face, like violence and chronic poverty. It also allows us to include their *cosmovisión* in theological discourse, one that contrasts with a closed scientific worldview, values narrative, and the extemporaneous public expression of emotions.

Hibridez also lets us understand the reasons and motives for immigration. They experience chronic poverty, violence, and hunger, situations that border on desperation. The lure of a better life allows them to dream the American dream. Every single time one of them crosses the border the American dream is born anew.

I will now examine the way *mestizaje* has been used to build theological reflection. From there we shall present a pneumatic perspective of undocumented peoples.

6

TOWARDS THEOLOGY: *MESTIZAJE*, *HIBRIDEZ*, AND RELIGIOUS SYMBOLS

Introduction

If we examine *mestizaje* and find *hibridez* to be one of the main components of its condition, we must examine religious symbols of the community to consider the way in which these can inform our theology through *hibridez* in the Latino community. I now turn to dimensions of US Latino Theology and look at Roman Catholic interpretations of *La Virgen de Guadalupe* and *Jesucristo*. I am doing so following the example set forth by Virgilio Elizondo. Immediately after examining *mestizaje*, he describes how this is carried along in the religious symbols of the community. I strive to do something similar with the difference being grounding the discussion in the Pentecostal community of faith. For this reason, in this chapter I look at Roman Catholic religious symbols. In the following chapter, I look at experiences of the Pentecostal community. In doing so, I hope to provide an emerging theology from the Pentecostal community through the preceding examination of *hibridez*.

Elizondo focuses on two powerful symbols. Roman Catholic theology usually follows this pattern. The first symbol is *La Virgen de Guadalupe*. She has many interconnected points throughout Latin America. The second is *Jesucristo* and his incarnation as redemptive. I wish to examine these also and try to build bridges to our discussion on *hibridez*. I also give an *interpretación evangélica* or a Pentecostal rereading of this particular tradition and strive to give a pneumatic contribution to our discussion on *hibridez* and *mestizaje*. Finally, I also examine Sor Juana Inés de la Cruz as a theological figure nurturing an emerging *hibridez* from Latin America. Because I am Pentecostal, I also make a pneumatological connection that through the Holy Spirit, God affirms the identity *del pueblo híbrido* despite their location at the margins of society and engages their daily struggle in *lo cotidiano* to reconcile them with *otredad*.

Religious Symbols: The Narrative of *la Virgen de Guadalupe*

La Virgen is a symbol with which many *Pentecostales* may not be familiar. In mainstream Pentecostal circles, she is treated as an aberration of the Christian faith. To understand this symbol's theological function, I give a brief summary of the *Guadalupe* event. I also include this summary to foster ecumenical dialogue and mutual understanding between Roman Catholics and Pentecostal communities.

The context of the narrative is the year 1521, after the fall of the Aztec empire to Spain. Many Aztecs were deeply affected by this rupture in their *cosmovisión*. For example, the natives' way of life was taught as being inferior to the ways of the Spanish *conquistadores*. The situation harmed the natives in many ways. In 1527 Juan Zumárraga, the Bishop of México, wrote a letter to the king of Spain describing the abuse, murder, and violence he saw which led him to conclude that the earth would go to perdition if God did not intervene.[1]

At the same time, Roman Catholic missionaries tried to do contextual missionary work.[2] Through these efforts one particular native, *el-que-habla-como-un-águila* (he-who-speaks-like-an-eagle), was baptized along with his wife. He was christened Juan Diego and his wife María Lucía.[3] The stories of Juan Diego indicate that he was a

---

[1] Eduardo Chávez, *Our Lady of Guadalupe and Saint Juan Diego: The Historical Evidence* (Lanham, MD: Rowman and Littlefield, 2006).

[2] Ángel Vigil, *The Eagle on the Cactus* (Englewood: Greenwood Publishers, 2000).

[3] *Nican Mopohua* (1649). Department of Social Sciences, University of California San Diego. 'http://weber.ucsd.edu/~dkjordan/nahuatl/nican/Nican Mopohua.html.' Accessed September 29, 2011. Nican Mopohua is interpreted in English as: 'here it is told'. It is the earliest extant narrative concerning Juan Diego and *La Virgen de Guadalupe*.

poor native yet a devout Christian. He attended mass on both Saturdays and Sundays spending the entirety of both days at church. Juan Diego was deeply involved in the life of the church. In a work by Fortino Hipólito Vera, several witnesses give their positive testimonies concerning Juan Diego.[4] He lived honestly and was qualified as a righteous and upright person. Furthermore, many attest that he was a Christian who feared God who was of good conscience and was always present for mass. He strove to live a devoted life, which Pentecostals would understand as a sanctified life. Juan Diego also had a faith informed to some extent by the Aztec religion including a *cosmovisión* that allowed for signs and wonders in his new Christian faith. In many ways it was hybrid faith that reconciled his Aztec *cosmovisión* open to miracles and the miraculous.

On Saturday, December 9, 1531 – ten years after the fall of the Aztec empire – he was on his way to mass when he heard a chorus of birds singing on the hill of *Tepeyac*. *Tepeyac* itself has great significance because it was the place where the Aztecs once had a shrine dedicated to *Tonantzin*, the Aztec goddess protector of the earth and corn. After hearing the birds and going up the hill with curiosity, Juan Diego saw a beautiful woman dressed in traditional native attire, who shared his skin tone, and who spoke in his native Nahuatl language. The woman then told Juan Diego who she was, *la Virgen Tlecuautlacupeuh*. Because he was a good pure soul, she had chosen him to deliver a message to the Bishop of Mexico, Juan Zumárraga. He was to ask the Bishop to build a church on that spot as a monument of love for the vanquished Aztec people – who she specifies as her own people – on *Tepeyac*.

Juan Diego went to deliver the message to the Bishop. Initially, the Bishop's assistants did not believe him and told him to leave. However, impressed by his earnestness they let him speak to the Bishop who was gentle with him but ultimately told him to leave. Nonetheless, the Bishop was also deeply impressed by Juan Diego's sincerity. Juan Diego left deeply concerned about not having fulfilled his mandate. *La Virgen* then appeared to Juan Diego again and told him to speak to the Bishop again. Once more, he was turned

---

[4] Fortinio Hipólito Vera, *Informaciones sobre la Milagrosa Aparición de la Santísima Virgen de Guadalupe Recibidas en 1666 y 1723* (Imprenta Católica a Cargo de Jorge Sigüenza, 1889), pp. 21, 27.

away but this time the Bishop told him to ask *la Virgen* for a sign. *La Virgen* then appeared to Juan Diego a third time and told him that his sick uncle would be healed. She also reassured him that she would give him a sign for Bishop Zumárraga.

On December 12, the *Virgen* appeared to Juan Diego a fourth time. She instructed him to go to the top of the hill of *Tepeyac*. Once there, Juan Diego found fresh luscious summer Roses de Castile. The sign was important because he found these roses in the middle of rock and dead brush during the middle of the cold and barren winter. It was not time for roses to bloom. Juan Diego put these roses in his *tilma* or native attire and took these to the Bishop. This third time the Bishop's helpers insisted on turning him away, but then they saw the beautiful roses he carried. They reached for the roses but as they lunged to grab them from Juan Diego these would disappear. Impressed by these events they allowed Juan Diego to see Bishop Zumárraga.

The Bishop also saw the roses. When he reached for them the image of *La Virgen* appeared etched on Juan Diego's *tilma*. The Bishop was convinced by this sign, repented for his disbelief, and offered hospitality to Juan Diego. Soon thereafter, Zumárraga petitioned the king to construct a new church dedicated to the *Virgen* on the Hill of *Tepeyac*.

Several theologians have examined the story of *la Virgen de Guadalupe* unpacking the deep layers of symbolism in this story. First, *la Virgen de Guadalupe* is a powerful symbol of resistance for Mexican–Americans because she affirms their existence as *mestizo* peoples.[5] She is *morenita* (or dark-skinned), when compared to the all-white religion of the Spaniards. In this symbol, Mexican–Americans can take pride in both their ancestries – European and Amerindian.[6]

---

[5] There are several texts that deal with the importance of the Virgin. They all come to terms with the importance of the Virgin as a symbol in the Mexican–American community. For more see Virgilio Elizondo, *et al.*, *The Treasure of Guadalupe* (Lanham, MD: Rowman and Littlefield, 2006); Angel Vigil, *The Eagle on the Cactus* (Englewood, CO: Greenwood Publishers, 2000); Maxwell E. Johnson, *The Virgin of Guadalupe: Theological Reflections of an Anglo-Lutheran Linguist* (Lanham, MD: Rowman and Littlefield, 2002); Eduardo Chávez, *Our Lady of Guadalupe and Saint Juan Diego: The Historical Evidence* (Lanham, MD: Rowman and Littlefield, 2006); Jeanette Rodríguez, *Our Lady of Guadalupe: Faith and Empowerment among Mexican–American Women* (Austin, TX: University of Texas Press, 2001).

[6] Elizondo, *The Future is Mestizo*, p. 35.

Even her name, *Guadalupe*, is a synthesis of Spanish and Nahuatl. When Juan Diego asked for her name, she told him that it was *Tlecuautlacupeuh*. The Spaniards heard this and it sounded similar to the Spanish, *de Guadalupe*. This was simultaneously important for the Spaniards for in *Extremadura*, Spain there was already a deep Marian devotion for *la Virgen de Guadalupe de Extremadura*, a black Madonna.

Theology and *La Virgen de Guadalupe*

Consequently, the *Virgen* became a powerful symbol that decentered both the Amerindian and Spanish *cosmovisiones*. She affirmed the Amerindian heritage including its unique medicine, art, philosophy, commerce, education, astronomy, and agriculture.[7] Elizondo, in particular, believes Amerindian ways of life were more humanizing: teaching proper upbringing of the young people, respect for the elders and their ways, and respect for the dignity of the other.[8]

In many ways the *Virgen* was a Christian symbol with which the vanquished Aztecs could identify. She spoke their language, had their skin tone, and dressed like them. She was also a bridge from Christianity to the customs they once knew and were now considered inferior. In contrast to the empire and the figure of authority, she was a feminine figure, and a motherly figure that nurtured and comforted the fallen Aztecs. They could now also expect healing, signs, and wonders in this new religion. Furthermore, *Tepeyac* was a significant place that had been dedicated to the female Aztec deity *Tonantzin*. *La Virgen*'s appearance in that location affirmed a *cosmovisión* open to signs and wonders and one that demonstrated the validity of their ways. Her appearance also confirmed a particular brand of Christianity among the natives.

Other authors, such as Néstor Medina pick up on this symbol and affirm her non-European roots. For Medina, *la Virgen* is the central theological motif as she is representative of all those traditions that claimed no link to European traditions. In such affirmation, Néstor Medina struggles to break free from what he terms as pigmentocracy.[9] He also strives to affirm the dignity and the right of each people group to be heard in considering Latino identity. For

---

[7] Elizondo, *The Future is Mestizo*, p. 35.

[8] Elizondo, *The Future is Mestizo*, p. 35.

[9] Medina, *Mestizaje*, p. 117.

Medina, *la Virgen* as a symbol proves that in order to do theology one must also engage the non-Christian traditions and roots, and how they have shaped Latino Christianity.[10]

Also, *La Virgen* functions as a positive symbol in that she encompasses the borderlands as that which marks the intersections of identities, cultures, consciousness, bodies, and peoples, a place of *hibridez*.[11] In her appearance, she was relevant both to *criollos* and *Aztecas*. As far as the Spaniards are concerned, they could also identify with her through their religion, her name, and tradition history. She was a bridge person speaking to both sides of the bridge.

Significance of *Guadalupe* for an *Evangélic@* Point of View
In Protestant thought, Mariology is viewed with skepticism if not outright repulsion. Apparitions – especially those of Mary – are not a significant part of the Protestant worldview or imagination. Also, the terminology of apparition is not very helpful as in English it connotes a phantasmological or ghostly image. For these reasons much Protestant thought immediately rejects this appearance. However, in Spanish, *aparición* communicates the idea of appearing, or a vision of a supernatural being. It is the same term used in the Scriptures for Jesus when he appears to the disciples as they hid behind locked doors for fear of the Jews in the Fourth Gospel. In Spanish, it may avoid a ghastly and/or ghoulish connotation.

Another concern is that most authors who discuss the *Virgen* do not provide a Pentecostal perspective. Potentially, this may lead to a pneumatological absence in their discussions. For example, Maxwell Johnson, a Lutheran, states that while the virgin may not be necessary, she is an important gift of love to the marginalized and oppressed.[12] While Protestants may dismiss the apparition immediately, Maxwell Johnson believes a closer look at this *aparición* can yield important observations for theology.

Johnson also provides us with a pneumatological link by stating that the *Guadalupe* event pertains to a popular pneumatology.[13] Popular pneumatology, in turn, is the foundational epistemology and

---

[10] Medina, *Mestizaje*, p. 117.

[11] Medina, *Mestizaje*, pp. 134-37.

[12] Maxwell Johnson, *The Virgin of Guadalupe: Theological Reflections of an Anglo-Lutheran Linguist* (Lanham, MD: Rowman and Littlefield, 2002), p. 4.

[13] Maxwell Johnson, *The Virgin of Guadalupe*, p. 85.

hermeneutic of the *Guadalupe* story.[14] Another author, Eduardo Chávez, states that *la Virgen de Guadalupe* is a gift given by the Holy Spirit to the church. As such she is part of the church's miracles, talents, prophecies, and charismas.[15]

Orlando Espín also mentions *La Virgen de Guadalupe* as a pneumatological expression.[16] For Espín, Mary is not equal to the Holy Spirit, but she is somehow related with and to pneumatology.[17] God is actively loving, accepting, and sustaining the world through the Holy Spirit. The Spirit acts maternally in the world.[18]

Espín also states that *la Virgen* was a powerful prophetic message to the church. She affirmed their identity in their specific context. This emphasis on prophecy is also a pneumatological dimension. It is more than a foretelling of future events. It is a message from God speaking for justice for the suffering Aztecs people. This is an important dimension of pneumatology that Pentecostals miss. If we examine the story of *La Virgen de Guadalupe* we can gain an appreciation of how God is perceived to work through this *visión* for the restructuring and transformation of colonial society.

For such reasons, it may be possible for Pentecostals to interact and intersect with *la Virgen de Guadalupe* as used by Latino Theology. *La Virgen* is an important symbol because the *aparición* could be interpreted as a *visión* generated by the Holy Spirit of God. Particularly in a context of suffering and poverty, *Pentecostales* understand that *visiones* are part of the work and praxis of the Holy Spirit in their communities, and one of several manifestations of God's charismata.

Consequently, for *Pentecostales* perhaps the most important element in the *Guadalupe* event is not in the *Virgen* as a symbol; rather, the significance of this event is in *la visión* and to whom the *visión* is given. In this theological move, the Holy Spirit is not only present in solidarity with Juan Diego and the poor Mexicans subservient to their oppressors, but the Spirit also protests against the oppression of *pueblos mestizos e híbridos*: the indigenous, non-European, and *mes-*

---

[14] Maxwell Johnson, *The Virgin of Guadalupe*, p. 85.

[15] Chávez, *Our Lady of Guadalupe and Saint Juan Diego*, p. xix.

[16] Orlando Espín, 'Mary in Latino/a Catholicism: Four Types of Devotion', *New Theology Review* 23.3 (August 2010), pp. 16-25 (pp. 24-25).

[17] Espin, 'Mary in Latino/a Catholicism', p. 25.

[18] Espin, 'Mary in Latino/a Catholicism', p. 24.

tizo Mexicans. The Spirit is present in the lives of the *pueblo*. The *visión* given by the Holy Spirit profoundly affected and marked Juan Diego's *cosmovisión* and that of the vanquished Mexican people. The Spirit affirmed their *identidad* despite their location as *otredad*.

It is important that God chose a person on the margins of society. Furthermore, through the Spirit's inspiration, Juan Diego speaks words of life on behalf of and to his community both oppressed and the oppressors, *Aztecas* and *conquistadores*. The Holy Spirit affirmed the identity of Juan Diego regardless of a ruptured *cosmovisión* and his existence in the vacuum between *identidad* and *otredad*. Juan Diego became the chosen mouthpiece of God to address both the oppressed Mexicans and their oppressors. This is portrayed throughout Mexican artwork in which the Bishop of the Roman Catholic Church in Mexico, Zumárraga, *kneels* before the peasant Juan Diego and his *tilma*. The significance of the head of the Catholic church kneeling before a peasant cannot be overstated. Another key concept that *Pentecostales* may understand is the sanctified life of Juan Diego. By leading a sanctified life, as many witnesses attest, Juan Diego made himself available to the work to which the Spirit would call him through this *visión*.

Therefore, a possible interpretation of the story of *la Virgen de Guadalupe* from a Pentecostal perspective points to the Holy Spirit who is at work continually inspiring individuals and communities and giving a voice to the poor, marginalized, and oppressed. The same Spirit who gave a voice to Juan Diego also affirms those on the margins of society and inspires them and their communities giving them space and a prophetic voice. This *visión* transforms *cosmovisiones* so that individual and community may live a new life altered and transformed in the power of the Spirit. This is a dynamic that maintains the dynamism of *otredad* and *identidad* crucial to *hibridez*. Thus, the Spirit gives *visiones* that generate multiple symbols for the community of faith that affirm them despite their location in liminal space between two worlds.

Concerns on the Use of *la Virgen de Guadalupe*

Nonetheless, Pentecostals have many concerns in how *la Virgen* is incorporated into theological reflection. The first is the concern of many that Marian devotion borders on idolatry. This is a concern for all *Pentecostales* in Latin America. People venerate her, and pray directly to her, while Pentecostals have emphasized they should seek

Jesus Christ first. Furthermore, Pentecostals are concerned about people visiting her images and statues rather than seeking Christ. Another theological difficulty is a possible pneumatological amalgam between *la Virgen* and the Holy Spirit, a step that could be interpreted to mean she is replacing the Holy Spirit.

Finally, *Guadalupe* represents a specific nationality: *México*. Thus, she is not a Honduran symbol, nor a pan-Latino symbol. Though she was made patroness of New Spain in 1754, the patroness of Latin America in 1910, and the Mother of the Americas in 1959, there is an inherent danger in using this particular symbol to address the *hibridez* of the Latino communities.[19] Potentially, *la Virgen* may become a totalizing symbol for communities that we have already discussed are extremely diverse.

Another problem from a pneumatic perspective is the institutionalization, totalization, and crystallization of a pneumatically inspired symbol. Symbols that may decenter may also become totalizing. For example, *la Virgen* may be an important symbol to recognize and affirm *los pueblos híbridos* of the Americas; nevertheless, such a symbol must not create a closed system oblivious to the continued gracings, workings, manifestations, and charismata of the Holy Spirit in the community of faith. In a similar manner, a recurring problem with the *Guadalupe* event is how it is remembered. This remembrance may have totalizing tendencies or idolatrous tendencies.

For these reasons, we must critique totalizing symbols and institutionalized articulations from the past that may become idolatrous. For Pentecostals, this means that there is the possibility of continued contextualized *visiones* and the possibility of gracings (the charismata) outside of one specific Christian group. This is not to minimize the power of this *visión*. Juan Diego's experience surpasses deterministic and fatalistic conceptions of history, creating freedom or *liberación*. Thus, there is a need for articulating contextual visions but not dwelling on them or totalizing these. This is one way of viewing the work of the Spirit in Pentecostal communities. In this sense the symbol of *la Virgen de Guadalupe* is something to which they may relate. A difference may be that Pentecostals recognize the

---

[19] Vigil, 'The Eagle on the Cactus', p. 6.

possibility of new visions, and continued gracings, manifestations, and the charismata of the Spirit of God.

Significance of Guadalupe in light of *Hibridez*

The *Virgen de Guadalupe* is a form of resistance to oppression. She demonstrates the movement to identify with the vanquished Aztecs. However, she maintains a delicate balance and demonstrates a perpetual movement between *identidad* and *otredad*. Her significance is that both Amerindian and Spanish people could identify with her. She was an in-between bridge or a connection between cultures. Through an emerging pneumatology we may note a *vínculo* (union or bond) between opposing worldviews. She both affirms and negates. She affirms those on the margins and negates totalizing tendencies. Thus she affirms both conflicting parties in this interstitial space. She is simultaneously Spanish and Amerindian. It is possible an implicit pneumatological dimension connects both cultures and establishes a *vínculo* that calls us to align into nonhierarchical and motherly connections, thus decentering totalizing tendencies. We are drawn towards pneumatological affective dimensions that keep us from becoming totalizing. Thus, *hibridez* in a pneumatological light could help us recover notions of mutuality through the usage of symbolism and pneumatological language and reflection.

Jesucristo

At this point, I examine another important symbol for theological reflection for the Hispanic community. This is the theological link of Jesus Christ as *mestizo*. This particular perspective sees Jesus' incarnation and radical self-identification with the poor, marginalized, and oppressed in the specific context of Galilee as redemptive. Virgilio Elizondo also specifies that God cannot be known unless we truly know Jesus, and to know Jesus we have to understand him in the historical context and cultural situation of his own people as *mestizo*.[20] This is the key for redeeming the *mestizo* identity characterizing the Latino experience. In observing the Jesus of history, we

---

[20] Elizondo, *Galilean Journey*, p. 50. 'Mestizo' is used here in the male form because it is the proper Spanish grammar for describing Jesus Christ, who took the form of male Jew. It is not meant to exclude females.

free him from oppressive interpretations and manipulations by those in power.

Liberation theology, in particular, highlights Jesus' identification with the marginalized and oppressed through his incarnation and specific context. For theologians like Elizondo, Galilee is structurally parallel to the location of Mexican–American community in the US. Galilee was marginal to both the center (Rome) and the margins (Jerusalem). It is parallel to how Mexican–Americans are marginalized by Anglo-Americans and Mexicans. Furthermore, Jesus' intimacy with God the Father serves as an example of how to align humanity's affections with the orthopathos of God. This orthopathos is a call to solidarity with the suffering, marginalized, and oppressed. Lastly, the Jerusalem ministry of Jesus implies a stance of confrontation towards unjust structures and the possibility of action or praxis for the people of God against such structuring.

Elizondo states: 'the systematic identification of Jesus with the poor and rejected of society might give us the necessary clue to the importance, signification, and function of Galilee'.[21] The Galilee principle permits Elizondo to draw parallels between the life and times of Jesus and to that of Mexican–Americans in the US.[22] For Elizondo, this functions as an important structural parallel to contemporary times because Galilee was a symbol of multiple rejections. This is a terminology that signifies Galileans were despised for several reasons.[23] *Pueblos híbridos* caught in between two or more cultures will also simultaneously find multiple rejections because of their multiple embeddedness.

I think that we must also discuss the refugees Joseph, Mary, and Jesus Christ who fled to Egypt because of Herod's ire. This is a rich source of reflection for marginalized community. *Jesucristo* identified with those crossing deserts and the *Río Grande* in order to search for a better life in another nation. This same Christ entered another country without permission in search for a better life. This speaks to undocumented immigrants who experience family separation and whose children grow up in an antagonistic culture. Jesus cares, *es mi amigo Jesús*. This kenotic step is important to align the affective di-

---

[21] Elizondo, *Galilean Journey*, pp. 52-53.

[22] Elizondo, *Galilean Journey*, pp. 50-66.

[23] Elizondo, *Galilean Journey*, p. 52.

mension of the people towards God. He establishes a divine-human rapport that does not stop only at an identification with the poor and oppressed. Rather, this is an identification that moves humanity to change their affections and align their lives in just relations with *otredad* because Jesus being divine became radically other. Even in Jesus' genealogy we see traces of his hybrid lineage. He was the descendant of several Canaanite women, such as Ruth the Moabite, Rahab the harlot, and Bathsheba wife of a Hittite.

The life and ministry of Jesus orients us to proper praxis towards the other. In his ministry he included a variety of people whose lives he touched that were outside the temple purity laws and some outside the nation of Israel. For example, he traveled to the Phoenician cities of Tyre and Sidon (Mt. 15.21) and he ministered to a Syrophoenician woman (Mk 7.25-30; Mt. 15.21-28). *Jesucristo's* life also opens up various intersections with the work of theosis or sanctification. He was not only concerned with personal piety. Neither did he become a mere moralizer. His words on seeking God's kingdom and his righteousness take on a heteroglossic tone. The word righteousness is *justicia* in Spanish. In Spanish *justicia* is used for both social justice and righteousness associated with spirituality and piety. In this manner, Jesus calls us to proper relationship with God and with *otredad* by addressing two dimensions of *justicia* simultaneously in heteroglossic tone.

Lastly, Jesus fulfilled his time in view of the other. The theme of the now and not yet is prominent in the Gospel of John. Jesus' time had come, but simultaneously had not yet come. He repeatedly states that his time had not yet come and that the hour is coming. Fulfillment appears to be in the distant future. However, the first time that Jesus speaks of the fulfillment of Jesus' *kairós* was when the Greeks began to seek Jesus (Jn 12.23). The hour came or reached fulfillment with the inclusion of the radically foreign, the radically other Greeks.

Jesus lived and ministered in the threshold, a place of convergence, between his Jewish identity and his emerging Messianic consciousness, which is a global awareness. Jesus *kairós* has to do with a relational reordering and a disposition of valuing *otredad* as much as *identidad*. Jesus' praxis went through a pathos that related to the centers of power (the Roman centurion) the margins (like the Syrophoenician woman). Both point to the fulfillment of Jesus' ministry beyond Judaism to the Gentiles. Jesus is not paying lip service when he says that whatever we did to the least we did to him also (Mt. 25.40, 45). Jesus states it with full authority because he did indeed become the least of them, as in a poor refugee undocumented immigrant. He truly can say with full authority that whatever we do to the poor, marginalized, and oppressed we also do to him.

Sor Juana Inés de la Cruz: *Hibridez y Mestizaje*

These theological symbols reveal *hibridez*, the dance between *identidad* and *otredad* as a theological topic. Latin American history appeals to the person and work of Jesus Christ as the one who identifies with their *realidades híbridas*. I now examine the methodology of the writings of Sor Juana Inés de la Cruz. She provides us with theology from the margins as she addresses the faith of her people through poems, plays, and letters arising through *lo cotidiano*. Through her *lucha* she demonstrates a peculiar sensitivity to the developing social order in New Spain.

Michelle González states that most theologies ignore or forget Sor Juana Inés de la Cruz (1651–1695) and that she is a precursor to Latin American and US Latino theologies including Liberation Theologies.[24] Sor Juana Inés de la Cruz was a Roman Catholic nun in colonial Mexico who wrote several poems, plays, and theological works. Sor Juana Inés de la Cruz demonstrates a peculiar sensitivity to her specific sociocultural location in order to explain the gospel to the people in her context in a way that they would understand. In doing so, she affirmed the people of her context and their location outside the center of power. In a culture and society with fragmented identities she affirmed their location in multiple embeddedness so that this emerging *pueblo* could make the gospel their own.

She clashed with the Roman Catholic *status quo* of her time. Perhaps the most prominent conflict was in the attention this nun garnered from outsiders. At an early age she learned to read and write. Her desire was to study in a university. However, her situation was one in which she only had the option between marrying and living in a convent. She chose the latter but did not renounce to her stud-

---

[24] Michelle González, *Sor Juana: Beauty and Justice in the Americas* (Maryknoll, NY: Orbis Books, 2003), p. 8.

ies or her writing, which was contrary to the aforementioned *status quo*. Her poems, dramas, and prose attracted plenty of attention. Such attention was out of place for a nun in colonial *México* and consequently clashed with the set expectations of the established ecclesial authorities. Towards the end of her career she was forced to renounce her writing and remained silent for three years until her death. Her biographical situation and the circumstances leading to her death are topics of much discussion and speculation.

I want to highlight that she wrote in the midst of several contradictory and competing currents and *encuentros* in colonial Mexico. Her writing includes allusions to these conflicts through the various people groups in Mexico: Peninsular Spaniards, European traditions, *criollos*, Amerindians, blacks, and the particular circumstance of women in a male dominated world. She identified with an emerging *metizo* culture even though she herself was *criolla*.[25] Her writings from her colonial cell of traditional and authoritarian power spoke powerfully to the people of Mexico. She emerges as a personification of interstitial activity living in the liminal space created by this *hibridez*.

Though I could emphasize all these dynamics and her work is worthy of more research (books have been dedicated to a study of Sor Juana Inés de la Cruz) my particular interest in Sor Juana de la Cruz has to do with such layers of cultural currents intersecting in her writings and yielding an *hibridez*.[26] The fact that she wrote as a female from the point of view of a nun was challenging because it questioned those wielding power and demanded an approach of epistemic humility and openness to the other. She favored theological discourse that was inclusive and tolerant of difference, an emerging dialogue of *identidad* and *otredad*.[27]

Donadoni and Houvenaghel describe several tiers of *hibridez* in her writings. These have to do with biblical *hibridez*, Greco-Roman and Christian *hibridez*, and even Spanish Christianity and European

---

[25] Theresa Ann Yugar, 'Sor Juana Inés de la Cruz: Feminist Reconstruction of Biography and Text' (PhD, Claremont Graduate University, 2012), p. 36.

[26] Chiara Donadoni and Eugenia Houvenaghel, 'La Hibridez de la Tradición Judeocristiana como Reivindicación del Sincretismo Religioso de la Nueva España: El Divino Narciso de Sor Juana', *Neophilologus* 94.3 (2010), p. 474.

[27] Lisa D. Powell, 'Sor Juana's Critique of Theological Arrogance', *Journal of Feminist Studies in Religion* 27.2 (2011), pp. 11-30 (p. 12).

traditions. Donadoni and Houvenaghel state that the Jewish tradition was exposed to several transnational movements that formed and shaped this specific tradition through *hibridez*.[28] There are also movements of *hibridez* in *la identidad novohispana* that she is navigating through her faith. The *hibridez* of new Spain was a *cristianismo híbrido* brought over by the Spanish conquistador.[29] Her particular situation invites us not to maintain the *status quo* of oppression and marginalization. Chanady writes that Sor Juana Inés de la Cruz invites us for a truer vision of the world by giving more visibility to marginalized groups.[30] She was always sensitive to the other but not as completely other, someone who was *distinta* but not irreconcilable.[31] Furthermore, she bridged the conflict between *identidad* and *otredad* in her context which was the colonial differentiation between the *conquistados* and the *conquistadores*.[32]

Loa al Divino Narciso

An example of this *hibridez* in her writings is *El Divino Narciso*, an allegory about Jesus Christ. Donadoni and Houvenaghel state:

> Sor Juana Inés de la Cruz reivindica la identidad del mestizo novohispano como una identidad también coherente, a pesar de las oposiciones internas que surgen dentro del proceso de la formación de dicha identidad.[33]

Luz Ángeles Martínez also describes different discourses from different or distant cultural spheres generating what she calls systems of exchanges and mechanisms and strategies of such exchanges.[34]

---

[28] Donadoni and Houvenaghel, 'La Hibridez de la Tradición Judeocristiana como Reivindicación del Sincretismo Religioso de la Nueva España', p. 474.

[29] Donadoni and Houvenaghel, 'La Hibridez de la Tradición Judeocristiana como Reivindicación del Sincretismo Religioso de la Nueva España', p. 459.

[30] Amaryll Chanady, 'La Hibridez como Significación Imaginaria', *Revista de Crítica Literaria Latinoamericana* 24.49. (1999), pp. 265-79 (p. 268).

[31] Amaryll Chanady, 'La Hibridez como Significación Imaginaria', p. 270.

[32] Amaryll Chanady, 'La Hibridez como Significación Imaginaria', p. 270.

[33] Donadoni and Houvenaghel, 'La Hibridez de la Tradición Judeocristiana como Reivindicación del Sincretismo Religioso de la Nueva España', p. 459. 'Sor Juana rehabilitates the identity of a mestizo new hispanic as a coherent identity, in spite of internal oppositions that arise out of the formation of such an identity'.

[34] Luz Ángela Martínez, 'La Celda, El Hábito, y la Evasión Epistolar en Sor Juana Inés de la Cruz,' *Revista Chilena de Literatura* 81(2012), pp. 69-89 (pp. 69-70).

The *Loa al Divino Narciso* and *Divino Narciso* use symbols and ideas that the Aztec people would recognize in her play.

González states that this positioning was influenced by Jesuit theology in the New World. Jesuits emphasized the establishment of a relationship between indigenous and Christian religions.[35] The relationship was characterized by attempts to discover prefigurations of Christianity in indigenous practices and beliefs.[36]

Sor Juana takes the spirituality of the Mexican people and combines several Spanish elements that affirm an emerging world characterized by *hibridez* and a specific *mestizaje*. For example, in the *Loa al Divino Narciso*, Occident and America are two characters who have not yet met Religion or Zeal. When the text opens, they are worshipping the God of the Seeds. They describe this god as the one who sustains the world. They are so devoted to this deity that they give the finest blood from their veins, or 'a bloody sacrifice of human blood spilling' (vv. 35-45). It is interesting to note they are dressed in full native attire and dance rhythmically to beating drums celebrating the grandioseness of the God of the Seeds.

In the midst of their celebration, Religion enters along with Zeal. These represent European Spaniards encountering Occident and America. Zeal and Religion are not only at odds in their relationship with Occident and America, but they also clash amongst themselves. Zeal is masculine, forceful, and competitive while Religion is feminine, loving, and reconciling. In this *encuentro* Zeal wants to force Occident and America to worship the Christian God. Occident and America tell Zeal that even if they are forced to worship the Christian God their bodies may worship but not their hearts and minds.

These are impressive challenges to the European idea of power. In her writing Sor Juana Inés de la Cruz introduces subversive currents of the marginalized natives. It may also be a reflection on prohibitions that she experienced, since she entered into a conflict with ecclesial authority about her writing. Nonetheless, this reflects the cry of the marginalized and oppressed in the face of totalizing discourse, such as the cry of undocumented immigrant workers who know the laws and about border fences and still come. Re-

---

[35] González, *Sor Juana,* p. 40.
[36] González, *Sor Juana,* p. 40.

sistance is personified in Occident and America. They resist in spite of authority, but not in disdain of, nor for a desire for originality, nor exclusively in self-interest.[37] They do so for the sake of *supervivencia*.

Religion contrasts sharply with Zeal in her approach to America and Occident. This conflict is a recurring theme in the *Loa al Divino Narciso*. Religion states: 'Abandon this profane worship ... follow the true doctrine persuaded by my love' (v. 110). Zeal also wants them to abandon such worship, but Zeal's approach is very different. At one point Zeal states: 'Die, insolent America!' (v. 205). It is apparent here that Zeal wields the sword, but Religion bears love. For example, Religion curiously and lovingly inquires: 'What is this god that you adore?' (v. 249). She listens patiently as Occident and America describe the value of the God of the Seeds. Only human blood could appease their god (v. 350). In a move to seek reconciliation and to build bridges and to allow an alignment of two contradicting *cosmovisiones*, Religion presents the work of Christ in the example of the cross, where his body was sacrificed and the blood ran for the redemption of the world (vv. 360-367). Religion's contextualization and building bridges with Occident and America cathartically move these to the point that they believe and are baptized as Christians.

At the end of this *Loa*, Religion and Zeal exit together with Occident and America dancing to the beat of wild drums and singing: 'Blessed the day I came to know the great God of the Seeds!' (vv. 498-499). This ending encapsulates the point that *Sor Juana* makes to her readers. All the characters, including Religion and Zeal, exit to the same polyrhythmic drumbeats, dancing in ecstasy, and praising the God of the Seeds. The God of the Seeds is framed in a new understanding of the Christian God. Occident and America have a new understanding of the Christian God conditioned by their understanding of the God of the Seeds. It can also be said that the

---

[37] Benôit Monin and Kieran O'Conner, 'Reactions to Defiant Deviants: Deliverance or Defensiveness?', in Jolanda Jetten and Matthey J. Hornsey (eds.), *Groups: Dissent, Deviance, Difference, and Defiance* (Oxford: Wiley Blackwell, 2011), pp. 261-80 (p. 265). Monin and O'Conner give reasons why groups will dissent and deviate from norms. One of the possible results is that those observing will identify with the deviants, especially if authority is perceived as unjust.

Christian God has illuminated their understanding of the God of the Seeds.

In another important move, Zeal and Religion experience trans-formation in the dialogue with America and Occident. Religion and Zeal have taken characteristics of Occident and America through-out this whole process. It is not only Occident and America who have embraced Western Christianity. The result is an *hibridez*, and specifically a *mestizaje*, in which a new identity emerges in dialogue between *identidad* and *otredad*. Sor Juana challenges preconceived no-tions of purity and blurs the lines between the two civilizations.

In many ways we have a celebration of this mixture that is a condemnation to ideologies of purity. Sor Juana Inés de la Cruz transgresses borders and revalues the scandal of impurity that dis-places a search for a specific identity. Chanady states: 'la hibridez es una fuente de creatividad, de autenticidad, y de renovación de es-quemas esclerosados ... Nos fuerza a hablar de la frontera'. She de-scribes the *la frontera* as an *herida abierta* where the Third World grates against the first and bleeds.[38] And before a scab forms, it hemorrhages against the lifeblood of two worlds merging to form a third country – a border culture.[39] This is evident in Sor Juana Inés de la Cruz. There is an emerging hybridity that is in negotiation, in movement. It is being thought out and defined and used to rethink and redefine Latin American identity or identities.[40]

Liberative Dimensions

In Yugar's opinion Sor Juana proposes an alternative worldview/cosmos as a model for humans to reconnect with na-ture, the earth, trees, flowers, the sea, and hills.[41] Such a stance is full of political implications. The intent of Sor Juana's poem was to equalize distinct worldviews in her social location.[42] Sor Juana af-firmed a Mesoamerican Christian anthropological perspective that values all of God's creation as beautiful and intrinsically valuable.[43]

---

[38] Chanady, 'La Hibridez como Significación Imaginaria', p. 276. 'Hibridity is a source of creativity, of authenticity, and renewal of institutionalized resistance to change ... It forces us to talk about the border.'

[39] Chanady, 'La Hibridez como Significación Imaginaria', p. 276.

[40] Chanady, 'La Hibridez como Significación Imaginaria', p. 276.

[41] Yugar, 'Sor Juana Inés de la Cruz', p. 117.

[42] Yugar, 'Sor Juana Inés de la Cruz', p. 117.

[43] Yugar, 'Sor Juana Inés de la Cruz', p. 126.

González also highlights the importance of context and social location.[44] Her central theme is an emphasis on contemporary context and struggles of oppressed peoples.[45] She lifts up the humanity of nonpersons: those human beings who are considered less than human by society, because that society is based on privileges arrogated by a minority are the forgotten masses.[46] Sor Juana Inés de la Cruz applies these considerations through an emphasis on beauty, or theological aesthetics.[47] She uses symbols, imagination, emotion, and art as her privileged expression of the encounter with the divine and its articulation.[48] González rejects a western rationalism that divorces content from the aesthetic. She states that theology lost its beauty and therefore also lost its ability to reflect the glory of God.

Popular religious practices demonstrate the intrinsic value of the aesthetic. These are demonstrated in popular Catholicism.[49] One cannot separate the reception of God's love from the socio-political embodiment of that love in social praxis.[50] God's beauty is revealed in the suffering cross and challenges human constructions of the beautiful.[51] This affective dimension is strongly tied to pneumatological reflections from Latin America.

Conclusions

I have examined three particular examples of *hibridez* in Latin America. The first is *la Virgen de Guadalupe*. She is a powerful symbol because she invites the reader to examine an emerging identity as both Amerindian and Spanish. She invites us to value the Aztec *cosmovisión* as an important contributor alongside the Spanish *cosmovisión* to the formation of Mexico. I noted that an *evangélic@* perspective may see her as part of the continued gracings of the Holy Spirit in the church. However, such a perspective must allow for

---

[44] González, *Sor Juana*, p. 8.
[45] González, *Sor Juana*, p. 8.
[46] González, *Sor Juana*, p. 12.
[47] González, *Sor Juana*, p. 13.
[48] González, *Sor Juana*, p. 8.
[49] González, *Sor Juana*, p. 160.
[50] González, *Sor Juana*, p. 160.
[51] González, *Sor Juana*, p. 183.

new *visiones* in the community, where God is still operating and fashioning a new humanity.

In Latino theology, the symbol of *Jesucristo* is also important. Virgilio Elizondo demonstrates this in how he incorporates *mestizo* identity in Jesus Christ. His identification is redemptive because gives the people on the margins a sense of value. His identification is also transformative because it gives the marginalized and oppressed a *visión* for a better life. I also noted that *Jesucristo* had a ministry that identified with the completeness of humanity. He identified even with those crossing deserts and bodies of water in order to get to a better place. He demonstrates patterns of *hibridez* ministering to a variety of people.

In the case of Sor Juana Inés de la Cruz, we note an *hibridez*, and specifically a *mestiza* vantage point where she uses the aesthetic and symbols to convey her thought. I also looked at Sor Juana Inés de la Cruz and her method in which she affirmed the identity of the Mexican people in her context. Through Sor Juana Inés de la Cruz we not only have the symbols, but we also have a particular way of talking about the symbols. She uses affective language in conveying her message and thoughts to her target audience. This affective language is conveyed through poetry, plays, allegories, and music. She embodies *hibridez* in her writings and as a person: a nun writing in colonial Mexico.

I have dialogued extensively with Roman Catholic perspectives. I examined some powerful popular symbols in light of *hibridez*. I have observed several dimensions with which I, as a Pentecostal can identify. Such include the work of the Spirit, *visiones*, affective language, and a radical identification with the poor. In the next chapter, I will examine a popular pneumatology and look at pneumatic peoples, in search of further material to contribute to the discussion of *mestizaje* and *hibridez*.

7

PNEUMATOLOGICAL POSSIBILITIES

Introduction

I have dialogued extensively with Roman Catholic Theology for most of this book. I now seek to make a Pentecostal pneumatological turn emphasizing the experience of pneumatic peoples on the margins in order to describe the work of the Holy Spirit among those on the most extreme parts of society in light of an emerging *hibridez*. If not explicitly then at least intuitively, *los Pentecostales han apoyado* those crossing borders. Daniel Ramírez, for instance, states that many of the immigrants who make the journey are of pneumatic traditions.[1] I also remind the reader of Jaqueline Hagan's estimate that nearly 25% of the immigrants surveyed were *Pentecostales*.[2] In the US, many church communities provide care and support for these immigrants. This nature of hospitality is something profoundly embedded in the story of *Pentecostales*; as such, their ethos exhibits a transnational character.[3]

---

[1] Daniel Ramírez, 'Call Me "Bitter"', p. 40. In this he describes many of the immigrants being Charismatic, a term that is inclusive of Classic Pentecostals and *Evangélic@s*, as well as Charismatic Catholics. The all-embracing terminology he uses is 'pneumatic peoples'. This is a broad definition including Catholic Charismatics, Classic Pentecostals, and Charismatics.

[2] Jacqueline Hagan, 'Faith for the Journey', in Daniel Groody and Gioachinno Champese (eds.), *A Promised Land, A Perilous Journey* (Notre Dame: University of Notre Dame Press, 2008), pp. 3-19 (p. 16).

[3] Ramírez, 'Call Me "Bitter"', p. 40.

In order to provide a pneumatological insight, I made the point that *Pentecostales* are not concerned with the symbols per se, but with an experience with God who is the giver of symbols. God reveals his *orthopathos* through these experiences, affirming and engaging the community in *lo cotidiano*, empowering them in their *sobrevivencia*. An encounter with the giver of symbols and *visiones* is a part of this analysis of immigration. The Holy Spirit works through a profound affective dimension to humanize immigrants through an emerging *hibridez*.

In this chapter I further ground theological reflection from a Pentecostal perspective, specifically through the description of the Baptism of the Spirit and the charismatic life in the Spirit of God. I refer to the Azusa Street revival, but I make this disclaimer: I do not think Azusa Street was utopic; rather, there are some considerations we must make of Azusa if we are to consider a Pentecostal contribution for theology from *lo cotidiano*. I also think there are more examples throughout the Southwest US about transcultural and cross-border movements in the Latino movement. I do not want to ignore the great Pentecostal revival that took place simultaneously in the US and in Latin America, as pointed out by Daniel Ramírez, who notes that there were many centers of Pentecostal revival in the borderlands between Mexico and the US.[4]

I point to Azusa Street because I want to stress that undocumented *Pentecostales* were present at this revival. I make the point that this place that is cherished by many was also a place where brown undocumented people were present. Thus, I wish to do away with the idealization or a sanitized version of this revival. The particular point of undocumented immigration in the US should also inform our historiographies and theology. Undocumented immigrants are a part of the poor and marginalized whose story has not been examined at length.

---

[4] Daniel Ramírez, *Migrating Faith: Pentecostalism in the United States and Mexico in the Twentieth Century* (Chapel Hill: UNC Press, 2015).

Pneumatological Identification and *Hibridez* in Azusa Street

In Azusa Street, the empowering presence of the Holy Spirit is a theological perspective that must be considered in a theology pertaining to *hibridez* and to the spirituality of the immigrants there. Several authors have given us a critical look at the revival. Gastón Espinosa, Daniel Ramírez, and Arlene Sánchez Walsh, for example, describe an inherent contradiction about the work of the Spirit at Azusa Street.[5] Theologically, the Spirit appears to be doing one thing; yet in praxis, this experience and the implied theological ideas fail to take root or to transform the ethos of the church permanently. I discuss more of this contradiction in what follows in light of these authors.

Arlene Sánchez Walsh, in particular, has examined the interplay of ethnic identity among Pentecostals and how these negotiated their varied identities in light of the revival.[6] She concludes that many Pentecostals had to choose between their own ethnic identity and becoming Americanized when they thought of conversion.[7] Sánchez Walsh's concern is how these early Hispanic Pentecostals negotiated their identity in light of the experience of Spirit Baptism, evangelical pressure, and sociocultural pressure. She argues that becoming a Christian for the Mexicans at Azusa Street meant laying aside their own culture and becoming American.

Although she is very critical of Azusa, Sánchez Walsh describes something else implicit in *lo cotidiano* of the revival that showed much promise. As we look back on it we see a glaring contradiction in the revival because it did not remain true to its promise or what I think are its experienced theological implications. The revival was

---

[5] Arlene Sánchez Walsh, *Latino Pentecostal Identity: Evangelical Faith, Self, and Society* (New York: Columbia University Press, 2003); Daniel Ramírez, 'Borderlands Praxis: The Immigrant Experience in Latino Pentecostal Churches', *Journal of the American Academy of Religion* 67/3 (September 1999), pp. 574-89 (p. 574); Gastón Espinosa, '"El Azteca:" Francisco Olazábal and Latino Pentecostal Charisma, Power, and Healing in the Borderlands', *Journal of the American Academy of Religion* 67.3 (September 1999), pp. 597-616; Gastón Espinosa, 'The Holy Ghost is Here on Earth: The Latino Contributions to the Azusa Street Revival', *Enrichment Journal* 11.2 (Spring 2006), pp. 118-25 (p. 121).

[6] Sánchez Walsh, *Latino Pentecostal Identity*, p. 1.

[7] Sánchez, Walsh, *Latino Pentecostal Identity*, p. 9.

material for serious theological reflection, re-articulation, and re-shuffling; but it remains questionable how much ecclesiastical and theological change occurred in light of the revival. I contend that the Spirit provided pneumatologically charged material for action-reflection or praxis. The Spirit was at work in a liminal and interstitial threshold between competing cultural identities at Azusa Street. Most importantly, the Spirit was carrying on a new work affirming the marginalized and oppressed in *Los Ángeles*. The controversy is whether or not the Azusa Street revival was able to produce a tangible change in praxis in the church and surrounding culture of the time, which sadly it did not.

For instance, concerning women in the church, Sánchez Walsh states that Azusa Street introduced 'submission to a supernatural force that affected both men and women, and risked democratizing male-dominated offices of apostle, prophet, evangelist, pastor, and teacher'.[8] The Azusa Street papers published by William Seymour depict men and women ministering, worshipping, and leading together. To the reader with enough hindsight it seems that the Spirit is fulfilling the promise of Joel 2.28. However, Sánchez Walsh argues that the emotive expression and the way women fell side by side to men was distasteful to many evangelicals. Furthermore, contemporary Pentecostal denominations and churches have gone back on such democratization. Many now seem to have taken to a fundamentalism that frowns upon female leadership.

There were also different cultural groups interacting in the revival. Frank Bartleman, in particular, made the statement that the color line was washed away with the blood.[9] However, this statement was an idealized illusion in light of the realities faced by the people of color in the revival.[10] Pentecostalism's attraction to people of color and potential mixing in churches caused discomfort. Consequently, these early Pentecostals did not reconcile feelings of Euro American superiority over their African-American and Latino brethren.

Nonetheless, there was a promise for pneumatologically inspired praxis, and this is my interest. In Azusa Street there appears to be an *hibridez* produced by the experience of the Holy Spirit. Different

---

[8] Sánchez Walsh, *Latino Pentecostal Identity*, p. 5.

[9] Frank Bartleman, *Azusa Street* (Plainfield, NJ: Logos International, 1980), p. 59.

[10] Sánchez Walsh, *Latino Pentecostal Identity*, p. 6.

people seem to intermingle in the formation of a holy liminal space relatively free from the pressures of surrounding society with an alternative *visión* of what it meant to be human and a member of the Kingdom of God. Furthermore, it seems that these were spaces where individuals were temporarily free from the bondage of super-imposed human borders. Nonetheless, I agree with Sánchez Walsh when she states that this implicit theology failed to take hold during the aftermath of the revival. Azusa Street failed to put into practice its inherent theological motifs concerning the multicultural work of the Spirit.

An Examination of Azusa Street in Light of *Hibridez*

I examine these contradictions because we need to look at Azusa Street with critical eyes. In particular, I highlight a specific people of color that were present at the Azusa Street revival – the other and immigrant peoples. In the material describing the revival there is a powerful dynamism related to the work of the Spirit in which these immigrants are accepted and cared for, but this fails to take hold in the everyday praxis of the church.

One example of this *hibridez* was William Seymour, the leader at the revival. He was an African-American male who was blind in one eye. In 1906 *Los Ángeles*, this was cause for curiosity as African Americans were excluded members of society at large. Another in-teresting dimension that the papers mention is the diversity of dif-ferent nationalities present in the revival: Russians, Chinese, Latinos, Muslims, and many more.

In the first issue of the papers, the editor describes how many are 'speaking in new tongues, and some are on their way to the for-eign fields, with the gift of the language'.[11] This is a reference to *glossololia* and *xenolalia*. The editor of the papers also states, 'this Pentecostal movement is too large to be confined in any denomina-tion or sect. It works outside drawing all together in one bond of love, one church, one body.'[12] There are also numerous testimonies from Roman Catholics, and people from different denominations, and even a 'Mohammedan' visiting and receiving the gift of

---

[11] *The Apostolic Faith* 1.1 (September 1906), p. 1.
[12] *The Apostolic Faith* 1.1 (September 1906), p. 1.

tongues.[13] The editor states: 'God makes no difference in nationality', for 'Ethiopians, Chinese, Indians, Mexicans and other nationalities worship together'.[14]

Evangélic@ Testimonies from Azusa Street

A closer examination reveals the presence of Latinos in Azusa Street. In one particular instance, there is a testimony stating: 'a man from the central part of Mexico, an Indian, heard a German sister speaking in his own language he could hardly contain his joy ... The only English he knew was Jesus Christ and Hallelujah'.[15] Later the testimony indicates that this man testified in his own language and the Spirit also worked through him to heal a woman suffering from 'consumption'.[16]

Many interesting observations can be made concerning this testimonial. For instance, this was a Mexican person participating in an English-speaking congregation. Furthermore, he testified in his native language. Perhaps this language was one of the many languages spoken in Mexico, like Chinantec or Mixtec. Perhaps he testified in this language because there may have been others like him in that meeting. Another peculiar detail was that this man was from the central part of Mexico. Consequently, he had not been born in the US. He was also described as an 'Indian', or a native Mexican. If he was indeed an Amerindian, it would mean that he was from a cultural group that had experienced exclusion and oppression in his own country through the colonial history of Mexico. Perhaps he faced that same contempt in the US and maybe experienced oppression parallel to what many like him face today.

These details are important to this discussion in several ways. The context of the time is that the government had recently passed the Chinese Exclusion Act. Racial and ethnic tensions were strained. Nonetheless, this 'Indian' was a foreigner who was able to participate in Azusa Street – a sign that demonstrated that the Kingdom of God transcended all barriers. Furthermore, God affirmed this man regardless of his language, race, legal, or illegal status in 1906

---

[13] *The Apostolic Faith* 1.1 (September 1906), p. 1.
[14] 'The Same Old Way', *The Apostolic Faith* 1.1 (September 1906), p. 3.
[15] *The Apostolic Faith* 1.1 (September 1906), p. 3.
[16] *The Apostolic Faith* 1.1 (September 1906), p. 3.

Los Angeles. It is reminiscent of Bishop Zumárraga kneeling before Juan Diego.

The Holy Spirit who inspired this 'Indian' created an alternate *visión* for his reality. His life was significant to God for the Spirit used him to bring healing to a person suffering from consumption. In a rather radical turn of events, he layed hands on a woman to pray for healing. We do not know the race of this woman; but if she happened to be Caucasian this might have been a reprehensible social taboo. During this same time period, Filipinos were beaten because they had married interracially.[17] The woman may have also experienced a molding and reshaping of her *cosmovisión* in different ways. The 'Indian' touched her yet it was not a sexual touch. Rather, it was a holy touch where God brought about healing, perhaps not only from consumption, but intrinsic as well. She may have received a prophetic disruptive *visión* to the metanarratives of racism and ethnocentrism. The Holy Spirit gave both the 'Indian' and the woman life-altering healing *visiones* of a new life oriented after the Kingdom of God.

Another interesting inclusion in the Azusa Street papers is an article written in Spanish that is included in the second edition of the Apostolic Faith. Abundio L. López and his wife Rosa de López were allowed to write their testimony in Spanish.[18] This is very important to notice because *The Apostolic Faith* was an English publication but this particular testimony is written in Spanish. I must also make a note that the following quote is taken exactly as it appears in the publication, with orthographical errors throughout. I preserve the original text as it appears in order to provide a glimpse of the rawness of the message:

> Soy testigo de el poder del Espiritu Santo, en perdon, en sanctificacion, y bantismo en fuego. Acts 1:8; Mark 16, 17, 18. Doy Gracias a Dios por esta combiscion y poder. Recibido de Dios conforme a sus promesas el os giara. John 1: 13-14. Gracias a Dios por la ordenacion de ir a la Calle de Azusa a la Mision de

---

[17] Mae M. Ngai, *Impossible Subjects: Illegal Aliens and the Making of Modern America* (Princeton, NJ: Princeton University Press, 2004), p. 112.

[18] Abundio Lopez, 'Spanish Receive the Pentecost', *The Apostolic Faith* 1.2 (October, 1906), p. 4.

Apostolic Faith. Old time religion llo y mi Espoza el dia 29th of May, 1906.

Por sanctificacion en verdad y gracias a Dios por la dadiba del baptismo del Eptu Santo en fuego, 5th de June, 1906. No podemos expresar en nuestros corazones dia tras dia y monento tras momento usandonos el Sr como instrumentos para la salvacion y sanidad de almas y de cuerpos y de cuerpos tomos tes tizo de estas promesas marabillas y miligros , en el Espiritu Santo y son promesas para cada uno de los que a Dios lleguen por medio del Sr. J. Cristo ... Due Dios os Vendiga a todos ...[19]

Abundio and Rosa López were Christian workers in Los Angeles who attended the revival seeking sanctification.[20] The couple testifies of having received the baptism of the Spirit on June 5th, 1906 in the Azusa Street mission meetings. They testify of forgiveness, sanctification, power, and Spirit Baptism. Their testimony is also later translated to English. Since this was an English-language publication it is surprising to see this testimony printed in Spanish. After their experience they spent time in *La Placita*, a historic Mexican location of Los Angeles.[21] They spread the message of Pentecost throughout southern California and perhaps beyond.

---

[19] Lopez, 'Spanish Receive the Pentecost', *The Apostolic Faith* 1.2 (October, 1906), p. 4. My translation of the above quotation is as follows:

I am a witness of the power of the Holy Spirit, in forgiveness, sanctification, and baptism in fire. Acts 1:8; Mark 16, 17, 18. I thank God for this conviction and power that I received from God according to his promises. He will guide you. John 1:13-14. Thank God for ordering my wife and me to go to the Old Time Religion Apostolic Faith Mission on Azusa Street on the 29th day of May, 1906.

[Thank God] for sanctification in truth and thank God for the gift of the baptism of the Holy Spirit in fire on the 5th of June 1906. We cannot express in our hearts how day after day and moment after moment the Lord is using us as instruments for salvation and healing of soul and bodies and bodies. We are witnesses of these promises, marvels and miracles in the Holy Spirit. They are promises for everyone who comes to God by means of the Lord Jesus Christ. May God bless you all.

[20] Gastón Espinosa, 'Brown Moses: Francisco Olazábal and Mexican–American Pentecostal Healing in the Borderlands', in Gastón Espinosa and Mario T. García (eds.), *Mexican–American Religions: Spirituality, Activism and Culture* (Durham, NC: Duke University Press, 2008), pp. 263-95 (p. 266).

[21] Mel Robeck, *The Azusa Street Mission and Revival: The Birth of the Global Pentecostal Movement* (Nashville, TN: Thomas Nelson, 2006), p. 189.

There are additional interesting observations that can be made of the testimony. There are various orthographical errors that demonstrate a lack of education and schooling concerning proper Spanish. These could be typographical errors, but they may also reflect the education of the poor and marginalized of Latin America or at the very least people who did not have proper schooling in Spanish in the US. The López couple testifies that the Lord is using them as instruments for salvation. God was working through them to bring salvation and healing to 'souls, bodies, and bodies'. Maybe the extra 'bodies' is included there to testify of the corporate work that the Spirit is doing in their midst. Gastón Espinosa states that this indicated a strong concern for a social ethos in the early Pentecostal vision of Azusa Street.[22]

Practically, there is a lot of trouble when combining services and churches of two different cultural understandings and languages. However, this union in the Holy Spirit was perhaps a lucid expression of Christianity to the people at Azusa Street. Robeck describes how people from different backgrounds, including the leadership of Azusa Street and Rosa and Abundio López, spent time seeking God at the altar and in Azusa Street's upper room.[23] Maybe they had a pneumatological model that could alter and reconstruct our ecclesiological models. The editor testifies, 'if it had started in a fine church, poor colored people and Spanish people would not have got it [the Baptism of the Spirit], but praise God it started here'.[24] Later on the editor again testifies:

> It is noticeable how free all nationalities feel. If a Mexican or German cannot speak English, he gets up and speaks his own tongue and feels quite at home for the Spirit interprets through the face and people say amen. No instrument that God can use is rejected on account of color or dress or lack of education. This is why God has so built up his work.[25]

There is also a testimony of Brother and Sister López 'helping Mexicans at the altar at Azusa Street'.[26] For Gastón Espinosa, this is

[22] Espinosa, 'The Holy Ghost is Here on Earth', p. 121.
[23] Robeck, *The Azusa Street Mission and Revival*, p. 168.
[24] *The Apostolic Faith* 1.3 (November, 1906), p. 1.
[25] *The Apostolic Faith* 1.3 (November, 1906), p. 1.
[26] *The Apostolic Faith* 1.3 (November, 1906), p. 4.

a significant event because a Mexican–American *cosmovisión* includes the idea of healing, and this is intimately connected to spirits and the spiritual world.[27] Azusa Street had a way of affirming this *cosmovisión*. Another account tells of the testimony of Brigidio Pérez, a Spanish boy who received Pentecost and testified of how God was now using him in San Diego.[28] His testimony is printed in English for readers. And in one last example, God worked through another poor Mexican Indian through the gift of healing.[29]

Sánchez Walsh describes that Seymour and Bartleman noticed the diversity of the mission and that it worked in favor of Seymour.[30] The heavenly language bestowed by the Spirit was a gift from above that allowed them to communicate regardless of their nationality or ethnic identity.[31] Pentecostalism liberated immigrants from the limitations imposed by language barriers and other enclosed spaces.[32] For Sánchez Walsh enclosed spaces refer to various dimensions of their culture but most specifically to the Roman Catholic Church.

However, I would also argue that there are many other dimensions that this may refer to. One of them could have been their existence in ethnic enclaves and ghettos. If we may draw parallels to the contemporary context, there are many human imposed borders and ghettos from which we eagerly await the work of the Spirit. At Azusa, glossolalic practice and pneumatologically inspired ministry seemed to transcend temporarily the temporal boundaries of human language and barriers. It could have also affirmed the working-class Mexican immigrant population *cosmovisión* of the dynamic world of the Spirit, leading to interactions with the radically different other, a dialectical process characteristic of *hibridez*.

The Spirit was possibly steering humanity towards God's orthopathos. This orthopathos could maintain a tension between *identidad* and *otredad* because of God's alterity present through the Spirit. *Glossae* were an expression of ultimate otherness, a divine protest against dominant discourses. It was an intentional drawing towards

---

27 Espinosa, 'Brown Moses', p. 266.
28 Espinosa, 'Brown Moses', p. 266.
29 *The Apostolic Faith* 1.1 (September, 1906), p. 2.
30 Sánchez Walsh, *Latino Pentecostal Identity*, p. 16.
31 Sánchez Walsh, *Latino Pentecostal Identity*, p. 16.
32 Sánchez Walsh, *Latino Pentecostal Identity*, p. 17.

otredad in order to change *identidad* and possibly mute dominant discourses. God the Spirit was drawing humanity towards a liminal space where one would demonstrate interest and identification with *otredad.*

Azusa Street Disappointment

What could have been a multicultural and multilingual promise for ecclesiological, social, and personal ethical formation was ultimately met with disillusionment at Azusa Street. In *Azusa Street*, authored by Frank Bartleman, there is a particular passage that is disturbing. He describes certain poor illiterate Mexicans who had been saved and baptized in the Spirit being deliberately refused the opportunity to testify. The leadership at the Azusa Street mission 'crushed them ruthlessly'.[33] Bartleman perceived that the Spirit tried to work through them; however, they were denied that opportunity. Bartleman described this experience as 'murdering the Spirit of God'.[34] For Bartleman, this was also in stark contrast to what had originally occurred in Azusa Street and was the reason the revival became 'more and more in bondage'.[35]

For authors, such as Daniel Ramírez, this demonstrates that what started as something promising ultimately failed.[36] For Gastón Espinosa this mindset led to a position many religious leaders took concerning ethnic and religious moorings. Espinosa is very descriptive of the mistrust native Mexican leaders had toward paternalizing or maternalizing attitudes of Eurocentric leaders. This led to a splintering of early Pentecostal indigenous movements and to the establishment of independent and closed indigenous denominations.[37] Espinosa states that as a consequence, leaders such as Francisco Olazábal remained closed to outsiders and took it upon himself and his community to train themselves in their own context avoiding contact with North Americans.

---

[33] Bartleman, *Azusa Street*, p. 145.
[34] Bartleman, *Azusa Street*, p. 145.
[35] Bartleman, *Azusa Street*, p. 145.
[36] Ramírez, 'Borderlands Praxis', p. 574.
[37] Espinosa, 'El Azteca', pp. 597-616.

Conclusions on Azusa Street and *Hibridez*

The Azusa Street Revival included two particular dimensions. First, it perceived the Spirit of God as His universalizing presence no matter the social location of the individual.[38] Secondly, their de facto hospitality flowed from an experience with the Spirit of God in which he affirmed their identity where the participants recognized in the *imago Dei* regardless of their particular place in multiple embeddedness.[39] Through ultimate otherness in the liminal space God affirmed *identidad* and *otredad*, inviting us to hold these in tension in a pneumatologically informed *hibridad*. *Glossolalia* served as a protest against totalizing tendencies and the oppression of the other. Such reflections challenge preconceived notions of personhood, ecclesiology, identity, and Christian identity thereby demonstrating the need for a pneumatologically inspired hospitality.

Amos Yong describes the importance of a pneumatically inspired hospitality and immigration when he states:

No wonder we are a migrant people, caught up in the migrations of the Spirit. Yet simultaneously, we are also an immigrant people, following the immigrations of the Spirit. But if the Spirit immigrates into human hearts, so do we, as living epistles, immigrate into the proximity of the lives of strangers, and there seek to take root, not in the sense of making their world our home, but in the sense of enabling the gospel to flourish deep in the hearts and lives of our hosts. Thus the call of the Spirit is the empowerment to take up and leave our homes and our comfort zones, to be guests of others in strange places, so that the gospel can become the home for us all. Herein is accomplished our own transformation, touched through the Spirit by the differences represented in the hearts and lives of others. The Spirit immigrates betwixt, between, and through our own diasporic crossing over (emigration) and returning from (immigration) the borders and margins that had previously divided 'us' from 'them'.[40]

---

[38] Ramírez, 'Borderlands Praxis', p. 578.

[39] Ramírez, 'Borderlands Praxis', p. 578.

[40] Amos Yong, 'The Im/migrant Spirit: De/constructing a Pentecostal Theology of Migration', in Peter C. Phan and Elaine Padilla (eds.), *Theology and Migra-*

Immigrants follow the leading of the Spirit, as they are involved in the struggle for a better way of life in another country. They establish churches, and faith communities and contribute to the North American way of life. Such a perspective may help us discover the stranger in our midst in a new manner. The work of the Spirit presents an immediate social dimension of this experience of crossing over and returning in *identidad* and *otredad*. It is the work of the Spirit of God to move us towards the other, to open space for a polyglot, polyphonic, and contrapuntal mass of believers. Pentecost presents a multicultural and multilingual opportunity for a holy and sanctified *hibridización* by the Spirit of God.

tion in World Christianity: Contextual Perspectives: Theology of Migration in the Abrahamic Religions (New York: Palgrave Macmillan, 2013), II, pp. 133-53 (p. 150).

8

PENTECOSTALS IN *LO COTIDIANO*: CATRACH@ INTERVIEWS

I now continue in this contemporary turn to *lo cotidiano* in a search of pneumatological perspectives concerning undocumented immigration. In this chapter, I interview Hondurans or *Catrachos* in the US in order to understand the undocumented experience and, finally, to do some theological reflection from that vantage point. I must say that I have hesitated with writing this particular section because the purpose of this interview is not to expose this group to any harm. Because of their particular immigration status in the US they may be exposed to deportation, violence, and racist exclusionary ideas against them. I risk a lot in writing but I decided to take this risk because my purpose is also to provide a more humanized understanding of undocumented immigrants. Overall, they enter the US in order to try to live a better life. Most of them present in the US are honest, hard-working people who are contributing to this society.

In the case of these interviews, the names of the people were changed in order to protect their cases and status in the US. I was able to establish a rapport with these people. I tried not to be too formal with them, as this was a key to allowing them to talk and share their stories. They were a bit wary about me interviewing them, naturally. Nonetheless, they were very eager to share their stories.

I was able to interview a diversity of Hondurans. I tried to be as diverse as possible interviewing males and females, young and old, as well as including recent immigrants and established immigrants. They all had one thing in common: they arrived in the US in an undocumented manner.

I want to acknowledge that I am not an ethnographer, or a trained anthropologist or sociologist. However, I try to be faithful to such disciplines, and I strived for my interview process to be methodical. First, I asked them each about their life in Honduras. Second, I asked about their journey to the US including the decision process they took to make the journey. Also, I asked them about their life in the US. This included questions concerning what they learned through this journey, and what they hope to accomplish with their journey. Finally, I asked them concerning their faith and the importance of their faith (if they had any) for their journey and their work here. In the case of most of the people that I interviewed, they came from rural areas. I could not find people from the same part of Honduras that I am from, Tegucigalpa. Most of these immigrants I interviewed were considered *campesinos* (peasants) in their home country.

María

In one of my interviews, I spoke with a lady who had been here illegally for over 20 years. Her name, for this interview, is María.[1] When I asked her about life in her home country, she tells the story of life on the farm. 'Nosotros teníamos una finca, sembrábamos muchísimo cacao'.[2] This also reflects the fact that cash crops are an essential form of self-sustainment in Honduras. In many cases, one bad year with little rainfall or too much rain that leads to flooding means hunger for the next year. María lived in a wooden shack, made from planks of wood, and they had clay roof tiles. They also had a dirt floor, and they all shared one large room in the house.

María described life on the farm in the village of *La Pita*. She is *Piteña*, and the nearest big city is *Puerto Cortés*. Even though she is a woman, she also had to work in the fields. They had all sorts of crops to try to sustain their way of life. However, she describes the great deal of physical effort in her experience. They had limited

---

[1] María López, interview by author, 17/04/2010, notes, New York.
[2] 'We had a farm. We grew cacao.'

tools and limited resources with which to scrape out a living in a very remote part of Honduras. Motivated to find better pay María dropped out of elementary school by the 5th grade in order to find employment to help her family.

Due to her circumstances, she worked for a wealthy family as a domestic worker. The desire for immediate relief from poverty and the demands of her job influenced her decision to drop out of school. She describes how she left her home in order to find a job to sustain her family. She would only see her family once a week for a limited time because her village was so remote. Transportation alone, in going back and forth, took nearly an entire day. María complained about the distance she had to walk from the spot where the bus dropped her off so she could walk to *La Pita*. It took more than an hour to walk to her house.

María also explained that as time passed by she got pregnant. This made her leave her job as she lived together with the father of her children. They had three children together. As soon as her 3rd child was born the father of the children left her. María was heartbroken as she was left alone to raise her children. To this very day she never received any kind help or aid from him to sustain her or the children.

She went back to domestic work to provide for her family. Her parents allowed the children to move in with them and they also tended the fields in *La Pita*. Domestic work was humiliating at times. She was a *campesina* and this particular family treated her with condescension making her feel inferior. She told the story of how the man of the house would like to drink late into the night. Many times she was awakened and summoned from her quarters to go buy him more liquor. She complained heavily to me about the drudgery of being made a peon for this family.

María continued to work for that family until she found work in the Duty Free Zone in *Puerto Cortés*. This was an area where foreign investors came to establish companies under permission from the government that would employ people for low wages and pay commission fees to the government. She ended up working at a *maquila* (a textile factory) for a foreign company in Honduras. This is a very common form of employment for the Northern Coast of Honduras as this is an area with many ports for large shipping vessels that sail to the US and other countries.

María became a machinist. Her task was to assemble shirts. More precisely her particular job was assembling the sleeves of the shirts. Sometimes she would inspect them discarding the ones that were not made well. This was a decent job, but it was not very well paid. During this time three of her brothers and one sister migrated to the US. Some obtained a US residence after the 1986 Immigration Reform and Control Act (IRCA) which granted amnesty to thousands of immigrants. After they gained permanency in the US, they began to insist that she join them in the US. She describes how she did not want to go. She had heard horror stories of immigrants making the journey and she had heard the difficulties that resulted in living in another country. Most importantly, she did not want to leave her children. She describes how over time her older brother gave her an ultimatum. 'Es ahora o nunca', he said.[3] It was then that she decided to leave for the US. María decided to enter the US without inspection because of her family's situation, and the lure of a better life via the American Dream.

María recalls the day she left. They invited all the church members to her house and they had a special church meeting at her house called a *despedida* (a going away party). They invited the pastor of her local church, a Pentecostal congregation. They enjoyed a good meal and prayed over her and for her journey in the power of the Spirit. Her father took her to the Honduras-Guatemala border, and put her on a bus to Mexico City. Her journey was difficult. She was worried because at checkpoints she had to provide the right documentation and she did not have it. In one instance when she was asked for her traveling papers she says she pretended to be sick. A compassionate Mexican lady persuaded the security that she was too ill to talk. Fortunately, she was allowed to continue on her journey. In Mexico City she stayed with a family that had met one of her brothers who lived in the US. They shared hospitality with her for one month.

After her stay, she took a bus to Tijuana where she went through more difficulties. Thieves stole all María's bags from the bus. All she had left was the dress she was wearing that day. It took her five days to walk from *Tijuana* to San Diego. Upon her arrival there she called her family from a public phone. They arranged her transportation

---

[3] 'It's now or never'.

from San Diego to her current city to be reunited with her brothers and sister.

She says she had so much joy to be together with them again. María said that they all lived in the same apartment sharing expenses. During this time, she was unemployed for nine months. She did not know the language or the customs of her new surroundings. Consequently, María's form of sustenance was to take care of her sister's children. Her sister, in turn, would pay her $100 cash per week. María used that cash to support her children in Honduras. Eventually, she began to look for another form of employment, realizing that $100 per week was not enough to survive and pay the bills in her new context. It was more money than she was used to yet she couldn't believe how now she couldn't make ends meet. María found work in the delicatessen section of a supermarket, where she worked for 19 years. She worked there wrapping and weighing cold cuts. Italians owned the supermarket so she learned Italian before she learned English.

She started on a salary $3 per hour and she worked from 7 am to 7 pm. With a more stable financial situation she began to consider bringing her children to the US. 'No podía vivir sin mis hijos – ellos iban a sufrir mucho', she said.[4] Eventually she worked enough to save money to bring her youngest son. Later she brought her two daughters. This was something she longed for since she had very limited contact with them as there was no telephone in *La Pita*. Additionally, in those days it was also very expensive to make that phone call so initially the communication was only through handwritten letters that sometimes took a month to be delivered.

María was happy to be reunited with her children. The first thing she did was to put them in school, but there was very little incentive for them and very little help. She tells the story of how she took her daughters to the public high school to enroll them and there was no one who would help her. She did not speak English and none of the children did either. She also complained of not getting any help from the few Latinos in that school. The picture that emerged from María was that of a helpless woman wandering around the school with her children trying to communicate with strangers. Unfortu-

---

[4] 'I couldn't live without my children – they were going to suffer too much'.

nately, no one understood or tried to understand. And sadly, no one helped her.

María describes that despite her broken English she managed to get her children enrolled. Unfortunately, all her three children dropped out of the high school during their first year. As I heard her story, I wondered at how ready they were for that experience as in Honduras her eldest daughter had dropped out of school by the 4th grade. This already put them at a disadvantage when they arrived in the US, since she immediately put them in high school. This factored in with the cruelty of teenagers particularly towards other teens that don't exactly fit in and probably led them to drop out.

Overall, María explained that her family had many difficulties trying to make their way forward in this country. She wanted her children to study, but they were never able to do so. When her son dropped out, he began to work at an auto repair shop. At first he was the cleaning boy. He cleaned everything and swept around the shop. After some time, he was allowed to fix a flat tire. This became his job at the shop until he was slowly shown the trade of being a mechanic by the fellow workers at the shop. He finally learned little bits of the job as a mechanic. 'Ahora es un mecánico profesional. Comenzó limpiando', she proudly says.[5]

She has experienced separation from the rest of the family particularly her home in Honduras. But also her extended family has gone its way after each one of her brothers and one sister started having their own families. Nonetheless, her children and their own families live together with her in the same apartment. They all share the expenses and utilities. They raise their children together. The rooms of the house are divided up among the different families. Different families stay in the different rooms and as her grandchildren have gotten older the older ones have been allowed to have their own rooms.

Her particular case is interesting because due to financial strains and low income she never processed her documents. She lives in the ambiguity of being here but being not really from here. She has limited education and limited English, but despite this her story is a story of triumph. Two of her children have processed some paperwork with the US government allowing them to work. Further-

---

[5] 'Now he is a professional mechanic. He started cleaning.'

more, her grandchildren are all US citizens. Her grandchildren are all in school and her eldest grandchild was in the Honors Program in her high school and is in the Honors program in University. This does not mean her children have been exempt from tragedy and difficulties. They also faced many problems.

When I ask her about the future, María states that her dream is eventually to buy a house here in the US. Maybe her children could help her. She doesn't want to pay rent all her life. Also, 'uno solo no se puede', she says.[6] She has never been back to Honduras. She wants to visit, but she does not want to live there. María exclaims that things are always terrible there. Everything is expensive. The currency has devaluated too much. She makes reference that the value of the *Lempira* went from being exchanged at the rate of 2 for 1 US Dollar to 20 *Lempiras* for 1 US Dollar.

I asked her why she came here. She stated that she came, 'para mejorar y ayudar a mi familia, para que ellos tengan un mejor porvenir'.[7] When I asked her what she would tell a person thinking of coming to the US she stated, 'que lo piensen bien, la pasada está terrible. Aquí solo se trabaja. La vida es bien difícil'.[8] I also asked her if she was happy with her decision. She stated, 'Mis hijos hicieron su vida, sus esposos trabajan, estamos más cómodos, no cómo Honduras. Estoy feliz, mi vida está hecha. Yo tuve un pasado muy triste, pero ya pasó'.[9]

Her Pentecostal faith has been very important for her during her stay here. She has been a member of the same church during this time. During the ups and downs and during the hardships that her children faced, the church has been the most consistent thing in her life. 'Jesús es todo para mí', she says.[10] In Honduras, the church was a refuge for her. It was also an important part of her faith during her journey. She gave a testimony how she was lost in Guatemala. She was hiding in a parking lot in a border town. After praying for direction a young boy appeared next to her behind a car. He told

---

[6] 'One alone cannot do it'.

[7] 'To improve and help my family, so that they can have a better future'.

[8] 'May they think about it well, the journey is terrible. In this country one only works. Life is very difficult.'

[9] 'My children have made their lives here; their spouses work; they are more comfortable, not like Honduras. I am happy, my life is made. I had a very sad past, but that has already passed.'

[10] 'Jesus is everything for me'.

her how much her ticket would cost for her trip and even figured out the exact currency exchange to pay for her journey.

In the US when her employers would not give her a fair wage for her labor or when facing discrimination from society as a whole she found a place in the church that welcomed her and made her a welcome person in the Kingdom of God. She is an active part of the community, but her greatest task is helping her family make it to church. She prays over them, watches over them, and suffers for them while they make their way in this country.

A humanizing look at María's situation reveals a woman that has experienced poverty in her country and poverty in the US. It also considers the push-pull factors that precipitated her journey. While in the US she has taken a part of a unique *hibridez*. She has worked in the same place for over twenty years and adjusted to her particular situation by adopting the ways of her new home. Her family situation is unique as several members of her extended family have US citizenship, while she has none. Her faith has been extremely important and she attributes her safe passage and the miracle of 'el niño que se me apareció' to God.[11]

Isaura

Later on I asked her daughter, Isaura, about her experience.[12] Due to her mother's absence and a father who left her family when she was only three, her grandparents raised her. She remembers from a very young age planting and harvesting cacao. Her tasks also included gathering wood for fire, planting beans, and maize when she was only seven years of age. Due to circumstances, she only made it to 4th grade. Upon dropping out of school, she immediately went to work in a *maquila* that she said was owned by 'chinos y coreanos'.[13] Isaura remembers that she worked there for two years. She was 13 years old when her mom decided to bring her into the US. She remembers the difficulty in making the journey. Unlike her mother it took her nine months to enter the US.

Isaura's journey was a story of suffering. She traveled accompanied by her younger sister and a cousin, a young teenage boy. Nu-

---

[11] 'The child that appeared to me'.

[12] Isaura Jiménez, interview by author, 17/04/2010, notes, New York.

[13] 'The Chinese and Koreans'.

merous times they were stopped and sent to jail in Mexico. After these jailings they were consequently deported to Guatemala. This occurred multiple times. In Guatemala she remembers her experience in a particular border town. As children they were not sheltered or protected by any adults. They were extremely vulnerable because they were unprotected children in a land completely foreign to them. This is a reality of many children who make the journey *al Norte*.

Isaura continues to relate how they slept in the streets. In many instances they had no food and they were forced to beg for their meals. Fortunately, she also stated that people would feed them out of their generosity; nonetheless, sometimes they would wander the streets hungry and go to sleep hungry. Many times they were locked in jails and were forced to share a communal cell with hardened criminals. They had no idea how to contact their mother or who to ask for help in these countries. They had no phone numbers, and no spare clothes. They were lost as children in a foreign country.

After a few months living in the cycle of migration and deportation in Mexico and Guatemala, Isaura's cousin said, 'tengo un número en la mente'.[14] He remembered a number he would try to call hoping it was his family. Isaura recalls the overwhelming joy and grief and the swirling emotions when the number they called was her mother's. They had spent three months on their way and her family was relieved to hear from them. Her uncle asked them what town they were in. Fortunately, he knew a Pentecostal pastor in that small town as he had visited that same town. He told them to look for the pastor's house and that they would be able to stay with his family there.

At the pastor's house they were welcomed and stayed for a month. During this time, they were taught that they had to act and sound like Mexicans in order to be let through Mexico all the way to the US. The reason they were deported multiple times is that they sounded like Hondurans. Just by listening to the cadence and accent in their speech the authorities could tell that they were foreigners. This provided the reason for so many deportations. They learned Mexican slang and the cultural innuendos.

---

[14] 'I have a number in mind'.

After spending time with the pastor's family, they departed on their journey with more resolve. However, their journey was extremely difficult and after another five months wandering through an unfamiliar country and being harassed in Mexico, they finally crossed the US border. Isaura describes how she and her little sister were harassed and embarrassed by a *machista* culture. Many times they were threatened and jailed. She acknowledges that they were very fortunate girls, for many women and girls are sexually assaulted and exploited during this same journey. Some of them never make it out of border towns and resort to life enslaved in brothels to survive in cities like Tijuana and Nogales. Some disappear and are never heard from again.

Isaura stated that she crossed a river to get to the US. They were told to take their clothes off, put them in a plastic bag, and swim across because once on the other side people would be able to tell that they had swam across the border because of their clothes. The children made it across without knowing how to swim. Isaura remembered that her feet never touched the bottom of the river. The children held hands with those who knew how to swim until they reached shore safely. Once across the other side they made arrangements to reunite with family. They were vulnerable and young. It is a wonder they made it through nine months with no food, no money, and no clothes.

Once they arrived in New York, they were enrolled in high school. Concerning her experience, she says: 'No fue fácil. La propia gente le da las espaldas a uno.'[15] She did not know English. And since she entered high school rather than an equivalent grade to her education she dropped out during her first year. She started work in a factory and ended up pregnant with her first daughter. The young man did not marry her and to this day never paid a cent of child support. Since the time she had the child she has worked to help her family. She would clean houses, babysit, and work in other miscellaneous jobs.

This also became a turbulent time period for her faith. She also remembers discovering new things and the temptations that came in with her new context. She would go back and forth exploring her new surroundings and comparing and contrasting these to life in

---

[15] 'It was not easy. Your own people give their backs to you.'

her home country. However, she remembers the church providing a safe haven for her. In one instance she describes being baptized in the Spirit. A visiting pastor preached the message of Pentecost and she received the baptism of the Spirit. She prayed in tongues all night into the morning. She prayed for everyone in her family in tongues. As she talked about this experience she noticed how this became a point in her journey where she became more involved with the church.

As I look at her experience, I think that this served as an experience in which she was confronted by the Holy Spirit. It also served as an experience that reoriented her understanding of herself in light of her situation in this country. In her tongues-speech she was not limited by human language or her lack of understanding of the English language. She became a person inspired by the Holy Spirit to become an active participant in her community of faith. The Spirit led her to a reordering vision for her and her family. While she spoke in tongues all night long she had repeated visions for her family and she prayed for all of them – her mother, her siblings, her husband, and her children. She offered different prayers for them interceding for them and ministering to them. That was an experience that marked her life so that she became an active part of her community of faith and a person of value because God blessed her with such experience.

She met her husband many years later. Since he was a US citizen, he petitioned for her and she is in the process of trying to become a US resident. They have a son together. When I ask how she makes a living, Isaura describes how her husband works and how she also works to make ends meet. Her favorite work has been babysitting because she got to see her son grow up while taking care of other kids. They have faced several difficulties, particularly with the current economic situation in the US. They have also taken in a teenager (her nephew) whose family did not want him. She currently works at a delicatessen like her mother. Her dream is also to have a house in the US.

She tells those who are thinking about coming: 'que no vengan. Que se queden allá'.[16] She also says that people in her home country dream of life in the US. They think things are easy but, on the con-

---

[16] 'May they not come. Let them stay there.'

trary, life here is very difficult. She is amazed that nothing is free and that no one does anything for free. To end the interview, I asked her what has allowed her to stay here and succeed. She states,

> We have always been in the things of God. We are humble, simple, but since we were little children we were in the things of God. We learned not to drink or smoke. We needed to have manners, to separate time for God.

She also states that she always dreamt of studying, and of having something of her own. She says that despite the lack of opportunity, she wants to learn to cut hair, and eventually get a diploma and have her own business. 'I want to improve myself', she says.

Isaura's experience is also typical of chain migration. Family members left for the US and eventually she also made the journey. The most difficult part of the journey was that she was a child. Several hundred children are caught on the border each year. Many of them do not even know where their parents live. These cannot be sent back as they may not even know where they are from in Honduras. Sometimes female children are exploited sexually, while male children are introduced to the world of crime, drugs, and violence. Another typical situation is that she had a Pentecostal upbringing in her native Honduras. This means that despite her perceived lawlessness, she is a human being with strong religious life and experience. Her particular story deserves a more humanizing look as she is not a criminal, but a mother, a strong Christian, and a person who is contributing to North American society. Her particular experience with the Spirit of God affirmed her as a person and as a valuable member of her community.

José and Silvia

I interviewed another young man that made the journey to the US at 16 years of age.[17] When I asked him about life in Honduras, he began to describe the many different things that occurred. He grew up in a very remote part of Honduras. He never once had shoes when he was growing up. He and his siblings were nicknamed, 'los chuñas', Honduran slang for 'the barefooted ones.' *Chuña* is also

---

[17] José and Silvia Ferrera, interview by author, 20/04/2010, notes, New York.

slang for a person without any means, money, or education. His family was so poor that they never got any shoes.

José also shared that he only got to the 2nd grade. He worked alongside his father who, though being poor, managed to work and ended up having several cows, a reasonable amount of land, and some horses. Unfortunately, José's father died when José was a little boy. His mother survived by selling everything. Eventually she married again, but never had the same resources. José ended up coming to the US when he turned 16. He says that in Honduras he had to be absent from school because he had to work. He did not have time for school because he had to worry about what he and his family were going to eat.

At 16 years of age José traveled through Mexico with his uncle who had traveled back and forth between Mexico and Honduras numerous times. They avoided all the main roads and slept in the open sometimes with cattle. Sometimes they woke up with their bodies full of ticks. They made really good progress until he got caught at the Mexico-US border. He was locked up by the Border Patrol and forced to report to immigration for a hearing. The judge let him in the US on the condition that he reported to more immigration hearings. José was very happy the judge allowed him to stay.

He describes his first few years in the US as very difficult. He got a job washing cars. As a teenage boy he was forced to grow up very fast. No one supported him – including his family members in the same city. He was on his own. He lived in what was considered the ghetto. Along with a wave of immigrants, he saw the city become revitalized with new immigrant presence. Once, the apartment complex where he lived burned down. He thinks it might have been because of the drug dealers and pushers who lived in that place. José mentioned how glad he was that he never got into that way of life. After describing this José stated how he had visited some *evangélica* churches here and there. He also made it clearly known that it was this that probably kept him from participating in illicit activities.

José worked and was earning good money, but he was deported. Since he reported to the judge and had been allowed to stay, his responsibility was to report to several other immigration hearings and appointments. The only problem was that the appointments were in Texas and unfortunately he lived in another state. He also barely made minimum wage and did not have any kind of family support to make a journey to Texas. Consequently, he never reported. In immigration law that is the worst thing one can do. One day, immigration authorities showed up at his apartment with a warrant for his arrest and deportation papers. He was sent back to Honduras. It was not a quick process. In fact, he lived in temporary holding facilities for months until he was sent back.

José was in his early 20s when he was deported. Upon his return to Honduras, he found no work. Things were just as bad as when he left. His childhood friends had all been killed, murdered, or assassinated. While he was in the US working, they had entered the world of *maras*, or violent gangs, in Honduras. None of them knew how to get out of that life. They all died. José tells the story of survival in Honduras. He did not have regular work, but somehow had managed to make a living there. In the meantime, he married a young woman, Silvia.

After some time, he decided to travel back to the US together with his wife, as things were not improving. To make things more urgent for them, she was going to have a baby. They decided to make the journey as José had done with his uncle by land. They avoided the main roads and had to hike for several miles. Unfortunately, Silvia could not keep the frantic pace necessary to avoid the Mexican authorities. They got caught multiple times in Mexico and got sent back to the Mexico-Guatemala border. After five months of unsuccessfully trying to cross Mexico, they returned to Honduras. Silvia lost her baby due to the stress and hostile conditions.

José resolved all the more to continue trying to enter the US. He came to the US alone and he arrived only in a matter of days. After working some time, he brought his wife from Honduras. Sometime after her arrival, they had a son. José works hard and earns more now than they would have in Honduras. They live with extended family who are also trying to forge a way forward. They see their son as their hope. He is an American citizen and has advantages that they never had.

At the same time, José is involved in a Pentecostal church. Their faith has been an important sustenance. Silvia started attending her current congregation when she found out she was pregnant again. She asked God for a safe delivery for this second child. After a difficult pregnancy she gave birth to a baby boy. She credits God for allowing her to have a safe delivery. Silvia also has dreams and visions given to her by the Spirit of God. José and Silvia also explained God's help in their lives on another occasion. Around 2 A.M. Silvia had a dream in which God was urging her to wake up because her whole family was drowning. She woke up and went into the kitchen where there was a strong gas leak coming from the stove. They opened the windows and called the landlord to fix the problem. They credit God for saving their family as the gas leak could have caused an explosion in their apartment.

José and Silvia represent the many young people that make this journey. Most of the immigrants to the US are between 16 and 34 years of age. They have many hopes in this journey. In their case, it cost them a lot. They paid a high price to immigrate losing a child on the way. This is very common as the journey is filled with danger. We can only wonder at how much poverty they were facing that they were willing to risk everything to go *al Norte*. Their experience includes family that are full citizens in the US. They work, worship, and make their lives in their new home, the US. Their congregation is a source of cultural affirmation while at the same time it serves as a place to process and engage with their new surroundings.

General Characteristics

A look at the lives of undocumented immigrants reveals the need to humanize the discourse. One of the most important dimensions in the journey is the push-pull factors that influence their decision to emigrate. There are many reasons why people make their journey *al Norte*. Immigration cannot be resolved through near-sighted over-simplification, stereotypes, and prejudice concerning the people who make this journey. In describing certain characteristics demonstrated through these interviews I hope to humanize the discourse concerning immigration. Each person has his or her story. They also state the adage: por cada uno que deportan, cinco más vienen con él.[18] There is a sense that no matter what the US government does, more will continue to come.

---

[18] 'For each one that is deported, five more return with him or her'.

Agrarian to Industrialized Transition

There are also some themes that were very common among their experiences. First of all, these Hondurans had little education. Of all the ones I interviewed, the highest grade any of them made it to was the 6th grade. In a society deeply embedded in the Information Age, they are people that may not have the necessary tools to survive. This is not of their own choice. They are part of an agrarian country, where one does not need an education to work in the fields. Many people do not understand why they need schooling when they will be working farms for cash crops. In the case of one of the persons I interviewed, Juanito, his family told him to stop going to school when he was in the 2nd grade. From that early age forward, he dedicated his life to working in the fields. That is how he made his living working the fields to provide for himself and his family. Here he does the same job he did in his home country only now he does it for a much higher wage. However, he has learned many new things including the benefits of computers and the latest technology. Here he owns a computer and is able to operate some of the latest technology with ease. Just because he does not have an education does not mean that he cannot learn anything new.

Another characteristic of these people is their resourcefulness. Though they have a limited education, they find many creative ways to make a living. In Honduras, many of the women were domestic workers. Over time, some of them began to branch out into small businesses such as a small kitchen where they sold food. Here in the US, they find work wherever they can. Their general perception is that they work the jobs no one else wants to do.

Overall one can find a lot of commonalities in their stories. Somehow their lives got difficult and their mode of existence such as farming became unsustainable. So in a certain sense they were pushed out of their villages, cities, and communities, and eventually their country. In Honduras, there might have been a sense of fatalism, but this led to a sense that their situation could not possibly get any worse. In their American experience it has led them to a very tenacious sense of opportunity. They are resolved to get ahead and find many ways to provide for themselves, their immediate, and their extended families despite limitations on work imposed by the US government.

While many Americans have a problem with the moral decision of violating US immigration laws, theological movements such as Sanctuary help illuminate the moral issues involved in undertaking such a journey. Sanctuary provides the resource of *lo cotidiano* by looking at the push-pull factors and the historical realities that precipitate their immigration. Furthermore, Sanctuary has also informed us that immigration is a complex moral decision. An examination of Honduras demonstrates that they make such a decision based on the contextual realities that fuel their desire of *sobrevivencia*. Any discussion that does not consider starvation, mass poverty, and violence that they escape is not considering the humanity or the basic *imago Dei* of these people. In light of crushing poverty where some of them faced starvation, they made the decision to emigrate. Their impoverished conditions take on a new urgency in light of situations where they work low-income jobs for pennies for the hour or where they are oppressed by their *patrones*. They have legitimate motivations for their decision to leave. They would rather work in a low-income job in the US for the survival of their immediate and extended family. The money they make in the US often sustains several families back home.

Finally, Sanctuary also has given us the idea that these immigrants experience an exchange. In light of the Honduran experience, several individuals may be undocumented for a lengthy period of time. This reveals that they have children and or extended family that have full citizenship but because of financial reasons or the lack of opportunity, they may not have processed their documents – a situation that is very common.[19] Such people have experienced an *hibridez* characterized by multiple embeddedness in which they live and cooperate with the North American way of life, but a lack of documentation estranges them from this way of life. *Hibridez* makes us conscious that they have experienced exchanges and have accommodated themselves in one way or another to the North American way of life. Their experience of *hibridez* locates them at a crossroad with surrounding cultures. Whether they live in a majority black neighborhood, or a majority Puerto Rican neighborhood, or

---

[19] Matthew Soerens and Jenny Hwang Yang, *Welcoming the Stranger: Justice, Compassion & Truth in the Immigration Debate* (Downers Grove: Intervarsity Press, 2009), p. 39.

in a majority white neighborhood, etc., they adapt to these ways of life and produce *variedades* of *hibridez*.

The Journey

The journey is always difficult, as Mexico has increased in the scope of its violence. Many of these immigrants are routinely robbed, killed, maimed, or held for ransom.[20] In the most recent violence, 72 immigrants were massacred in Tamaulipas, Mexico, because they refused to work as drug mules. Overall, Hondurans are some of the peoples that are experiencing violence in Mexico. They are often times pushed to extremes and suffer unmentionable injustice.

Particularly for women and children this is a perilous journey. Some of the women I interviewed painfully shared their stories of being sexually assaulted even by their supposed caretakers. In one case a young woman shared how she was violated in a jail in Mexico. It is a miracle she did not become a *desaparecida* or that she did not end up in a brothel. The coyotes, bandits, gangs, and *maras* make this an especially dangerous journey for women and children. Women and children are the most vulnerable immigrants. These suffer at the hands of corrupt adults. A young man that I interviewed says he has not heard from his sister since the time that she made the journey here. It has been over ten years and no one knows her whereabouts. Many families tell of the story of relatives that made the journey and were never heard from again. The reasons for such disappearances remain unsolved mysteries. In tragic cases they may be found as anonymous cadavers in the US-Mexico borderlands. Others fall prey to different types of predators.

The American Dream / Nightmare

For those who make it to the US their outlook is full of expectancy. Soon, however, they may realize that they must work hard to make it in this country. The American saying that they enjoyed quoting is, 'there is no free lunch'. Work does not stop and they have the responsibility to send money back home. Some send 150 per week, others around 400 per month. There is no set amount and each sends different amounts. Some said they only wanted to come for a month or two; however, they end up staying a lifetime. Very few of

---

[20] 'Identificadas 31 Victimas de Masacre en Tamaulipas', *Terra*, http://www.terra.com.mx/noticias/articulo/948152/Identificadas+31+victimas+de+masacre+en+Tamaulipas.htm (accessed August 26, 2010).

their original intentions were exclusively to stay. In contrast they have stayed in the US indefinitely. They seem to prefer the limited cash flow to none.

Furthermore, they tend to settle around established Hispanic/Latin@ communities from which they also face exclusion because of their 'illegal' status. Other Hispanics/Latin@s exclude them in other settings such as schools. There is also the problem of ethnocentrism among Hispanics/Latin@s. There is a tension especially with those who have recently arrived. In school this means that young immigrants often suffer the most problems especially with feelings that they do not really belong. For these and other reasons, they may prefer to drop out and work turning to what is a practical and visceral reality.

Though they have dreams, these seemed to be postponed, and are not often fulfilled until the 2nd or 3rd generation grows up in the US. Most of them express that they wanted to go back home and did not want an extended stay here. Some of them wanted an education for themselves or for their children. But dreams have often lacked substance. They lack the resources, education, or knowledge to make these dreams possible. For this and several other reasons they may turn to a gritty dimension for work and life. Many do not know the way forward because no one has ever devoted the time or energy to show them.

The Decision to Emigrate
Their message to those who want to come to the US is:

> Let them stay. But if they come here they must be ready. People think that life is easy here. It is not. This place is full of difficult times. Nothing is free here. There is no time. The pace of life is hard. We go through many difficulties.[21]

They also echo a common theme that if they had the chance to tell Americans why they came, they would say that they came here to work, not to take anything from them or to drain the system. Of all the people I interviewed most of them were working and making a living for themselves. All of them said they came to work and to provide for their families back home. Single mothers, in particular,

---

[21] María López, interview by author.

faced extreme hardships; and, consequently, they were forced to depend on government subsidies.

Their decision to emigrate reveals the nature of their decision-making. They are group/community oriented and willing to sacrifice for their families, immediate and extended. Undocumented immigration for many enabled them to create an alternate vision for life. It is not just a dreamscape caught up in unrealistic expectations, but a world that involves the concrete, actual reality, with all its viscerality. Proper praxis and action sometimes requires immigration. In a world with little or no options, it is a valiant decision to face that which no one wants to face. It is the height of self-determination to cross boundaries, and face discrimination in order to improve one's quality of life. An extended discussion on undocumented immigration is not a matter of relativizing morality and a question of ethics because these people understand that it is a matter of life and death. Every time one of them crosses the border, the American Dream is born anew.

We may now look at issues that drive them out of Latin America, and work for justice. We may look for problems and incipient racism and adjustments they make when entering the US. We may treat them as brothers and sisters and not merely as law-breakers. We must listen to their stories. For example, one of the issues that sets off immigration to the US is violence and instability in their countries of origin. This should also include more investigation concerning the effects of the drug trade in Honduras. Honduras is in a state of insecurity in which criminals and violent murderers enjoy a morbid impunity. In 2011 there were several intimidation attempts at newspapers with drive by shootings. There have also been murders of lawyers and judges in the country. Such conditions lead to a general underlying fear and makes the lure of staying in the US more appealing. In 2011 Honduras was found to be the most violent nation in the world.[22] A Honduran newspaper, *La Prensa*, estimates that 500,000 Hondurans live under the threat of extortion-

---

[22] 'Global Study on Homicide 2011: Trends, Contexts, Data', United Nations Office on Drugs and Crime, http://www.unodc.org/documents/data-and-analysis/statistics/Homicide/Globa_study_on_homicide_2011_web.pdf (accessed January 2012).

ists.[23] The same newspaper also ran a story where *Chamelecón*, a city close to San Pedro Sula, is a ghost town because of violence.[24] Most of its residents have emigrated and left properties and homes sitting in disrepair.

Theological Material for Reflection

Their situation raises many possible topics of discussion. First of all, there are questions concerning the macrocosm of their existence in the US. In the biblical text we find the example of the God of the poor who sent his people crossing the desert into the Promised Land. God sojourned with the immigrant. In our context these are some of the most marginalized and oppressed peoples. God numerous times said, do not oppress the alien for you yourselves were aliens. It is a repeated call to remember the status and social location from which they emerged – a location many North American Christians seem to have forgotten.

There are also other questions concerning *la lucha* and *supervivencia*. These pertain to globalization, fair wages around the world, and fair trade. As coffee, cacao, and banana prices drop, they decide to emigrate. Immigration is a phenomenon also tied to inflation, and the increase of the cost of living. One cannot pass judgment on these people without considering the context they come from. Again, the push-pull factors that cause mass exoduses from Latin America to the nations North and beyond must be considered in order to act justly in this situation.

Furthermore, we must consider their experience of immigration. For some of these immigrants, their decision to leave means a trip through the desert. They face a difficult environment, where they may die of thirst or starvation. They also face difficulties with predator coyotes. Some are the victims of kidnappings, violence, rape, and even slavery. Yet this risk is worth the journey to the US. In the midst of these difficulties there is an enduring sense of hope. They

---

[23] 'Hay Medio Millón de Hondureños Secuestrados por Maras', *La Prensa*, http://www.laprensa.hn/Secciones-Principales/Honduras/Apertura/Hay-medio -millon-de-hondurenos-secuestrados-por-maras (accessed May 7, 2013).

[24] 'La Guerra Volvió a Chamelecón', http://www.laprensa.hn/Secciones-Principales/Honduras/Apertura/La-guerra-volvio-a-Chamelecon-las-maras-rom pen-la-tregua *La Prensa* (accessed May 7, 2013).

make a living here as sojourners. They endure suffocating oppression in the US yet it is nothing when compared to the reality they have left behind since they are a broken and crushed people seeking hope.

One final common thread in these interviews was the presence of pneumatic religion among these immigrants. Most of them were either Roman Catholic or *evangélic@s*. Particularly in the case of the *evangélic@s*, their vision of their faith was not an otherworldly *oferta religiosa*, but of a God who endows them with alternate visions of life and who relates to their suffering. He is a God who heals their ills and wounds whether this is the trauma of having to leave their communities, of the journey, or of having to adjust to a new life in the US. Many of those interviewed were active participants in their communities of faith. These are communities where they are affirmed and in which they are made active participants regardless of the things society says about them.

In one instance, *la Hermana* Petra, testified of how God used her life.[25] She is a believer who has experienced the baptism of the Spirit. On one occasion she described how one of the persons that hired her to clean his family's house was extremely ill with cancer. With her limited Spanish she asked him if she could pray for him. Desperate and out of solutions the gentleman allowed Petra to pray for him. Over time he gradually grew better and eventually was healed. Petra describes how she later found Bibles in the man's home and other devotional material. He later started having a weekly Bible study at his house. She no longer works cleaning houses. But she remembers how God was able to use her life to minister to a person to whom she may have been seen as a mere 'cleaning lady'. It is this type of existence produced by the experienced presence of the Spirit of God that we shall explore in the next two chapters.

Conclusion

Looking back to this point we recognize Virgilio Elizondo made the valuable contribution of *mestizaje*, using it as the key to understanding the Mexican–American people.[26] María Isasi-Díaz later introduced the theological concept of *lo cotidiano* as a valuable theological

---

[25] Petra Ramírez, interview by author, 10/11/2010, notes, New York.
[26] Elizondo, *The Future is Mestizo*, p. 25.

resource. This allowed her to expand on the concept of *mestizaje*, allowing other people groups and nationalities to be covered in understanding a collective Hispanic/Latin@ identity. We demonstrated how in this identity there is a tension of *identidad* and *otredad* characteristic of *hibridez*. This reveals tensions in multiple embeddedness. *Hibridez* is a methodological principle revealing the tension between *identidad* and *otredad*. It is also a question of identity that reveals the nature of existence in this an interstitial space. I have examined this particular tension emerging from an understanding of *hibridez*: l@s inmigrantes *indoucumentad@s*. Any discussion on *hibridez*, *mestizaje*, or *mestizajes*, must always include a back-and-forth movement between the center and the margins, *identidad* and *otredad*, such as being *mestizo* and other groups on the margins of *mestizaje*, such as indigenous people, and/or also the *campesinas/os* of Latin America, who in turn may also compose *indocumentad@s* in the US. This exploration of *mestizaje* and the consequent emerging hibridez has revealed nuanced tensions between *identidad* and *otredad*.

Hibridez as considered from the experience of *l@s indocumentad@s* reveals that these are not only misunderstood but that they are also a violated people.[27] Behind mainstream culture's perceived ignorance and lawlessness, lies a deeply seated frustration of the consequences of the colonial legacy: violence, oppression, abandonment, poverty, and exploitation. Elizondo states concerning Hispanics/Latin@s: 'acceptance and passive resistance are the only ways to survive the present'.[28] I would add to his point that an active resistance would include immigration both documented and undocumented. Once in the US the only option for immigrants to survive and to prepare for an ultimate liberation is to accept their situation as it is and make the best of it.[29] To accept it does not mean they like it or enjoy it; it is simply a way of coping with it in order to survive.[30] Finally, the work of the Spirit in their midst cannot be studied outside the context of asphyxiating and dehumanizing poverty, violence, and suffering. Any attempts to talk of their situation theologically or politically without referring to these are nonsensical.

---

[27] Elizondo, *The Future is Mestizo*, p. 29.
[28] Elizondo, *The Future is Mestizo*, p. 29.
[29] Elizondo, *The Future is Mestizo*, p. 31.
[30] Elizondo, *The Future is Mestizo*, p. 31.

9

PNEUMATOLOGICAL REFLECTIONS IN LIGHT OF *HIBRIDEZ*

Introduction

I sum up where we have been in order to tie up loose ends and understand where we are going. In light of the above interviews, I shall examine an emerging theology from *lo cotidiano*. I shall give special consideration to *mestizaje* and *hibridez* in the lives of these individuals and communities of faith. My particular interest is in the work of the Holy Spirit in interstitial spaces. I hope to establish an emerging theological construct from the lives of undocumented immigrants who happen to be Pentecostals from Honduras. Their particular faith in their particular social location is a resource for theological reflection.

Summary and the Current Location

My starting point was *mestizaje*. It is the most important theological term for the Latino community in the US because it serves as the *locus theologicus* of the community. In its grounding in *lo cotidiano* we can do theological work for the people. In the case of many Latino communities in the US we enter a process of action-reflection in light of the experiences from *lo cotidiano*.

I also note that if *mestizaje* is our starting point we must acknowledge some of its shortcomings if we continue using it as a general adjective for Latinos in the US. First, it may be a term that strives for a harmonious whole and may not contain the entire Latino experience. As we have seen, Latin America is extremely diverse. The people who enter the US from Latin America are equally diverse. *Mestizaje* speaks of a commonality of experiences, but it does not speak exhaustively for all Latinos in the US or the people of Latin America. This reveals a continual need to nuance its intra-Latino tension and even tensions from the Latino center to those outside of this community. Latinos are diverse in such a way that *mestizaje* can hinder our discussion because it may refer to a narrow slice of racial typology or socioeconomic experience and it results in difficulties in trying to use it as an identity marker.

Second, another shortcoming of *mestizaje* is that it has been used by predominant Roman Catholic theologies and has been tied most strongly to the Mexican–American experience in the US. However, it is a concept that is experiencing expansion through engagement by Protestants and several different nationalities present in the US in non-traditional ways, such are the examples of Néstor Medina and Manuel Vásquez. This is also relevant because Salvadorans are surpassing Cubans in terms of population in the US.[1] According to the same statistics Dominicans will also surpass Cubans in the near future. If we are to do work for the community and we are in dialogue with the great diversity that the terminology Latino encompasses, we must recognize other Latinos in the US.

I state all this to make the following points. First, some nontraditional locations include Pentecostalism and undocumented immigration. Pentecostalism is underrepresented in the religious community and in discussions of *mestizaje*. Second, I am concerned about the omission of undocumented immigrants in this theology. Both are mentioned minimally and must be developed organically in theologies using *mestizaje*. In the current political climate undocumented immigration in particular is one of those polarizing topics that deserves much more discussion than the current rhetoric that is applied to it. We can change the discussion and the way we approach the topic and discussion.

---

[1] Mark Hugo López and Ana González Barrera, 'Salvadorans May Soon Replace Cubans as Third-Largest Hispanic Group', in Pew Research Center, http://www.pewresearch.org/fact-tank/2013/06/19/salvadorans-may-soon-rep lce-cubans-as-third-largest-u-s-hispanic-group/ (accessed June 9, 2013).

For these compelling reasons, I followed Isasi-Díaz's discussion on *mestizaje* and how she expanded this theological term to include *mulatez* and *mujerista* theologies. She pointed to the importance of *lo cotidiano* to build theology from or for the Latino community in the US. In expanding her meaning she demonstrated a great awareness for diversity within Latinos in the US. I also want to follow this example to gain an understanding of why many people from Latin America may enter here without proper documentation.

Despite the ideas of *la lucha* and *supervivencia* arising from *lo cotidiano* I think Latino theologians must include undocumented immigration as a pertinent topic arising from this location. We may discuss it without collapsing the argument into political rants about rights and ethics. I think that in nuancing *mestizaje* we may gain a better understanding of the Latino community and a humanizing look at the ones who enter the US without proper documentation. It further leads us to a robust analysis of this reality theologically. I think it is important because if we examine undocumented immigration we see the great disparity and suffering of the poor in Latin America. It also ties in to continued experiences of marginalization in the US.

If we look at this experience and the work of the church in the midst of such an existence on the margins of North American society we notice a strong Christian presence among these people, Roman Catholic and Pentecostal. This Christian presence should lead to a robust theology arising from *lo cotidiano*. In what follows I propose an emerging theology that moves between the pneumatological themes of the immanence of God and the transcendence of God as a matrix for action-reflection. In doing so we are taking *lo cotidiano* inspired by *mestizaje* seriously.

In many ways trying to understand the nature of God in light of *mestizaje*, *lo cotidiano*, and *hibridez* leads to a revision of the divine attributes much like Samuel Soliván's work in *The Spirit, Pathos, and Liberation*.[2] In his text Soliván makes room for the Latino experience of marginalization and God's orthopathos. He strongly critiques the traditional formulation of the impassibility of God. I think that in light of *lo cotidiano* and the *encuentros* of *indocumentados* and *pentecostales*

---

[2] Samuel Soliván, *The Spirit, Pathos, and Liberation* (JPTSup 14; Sheffield: Sheffield Academic Press, 1998).

this necessarily includes also a tension between the immanence of God and the transcendence of God. This dialogue between these two lead us to notice that these mirror tensions between *identidad* and *otredad* or a form of *hibridez* that could serve as a model of a just relationality.

At this juncture I also emphasize Pentecostalism. Pentecostalism has grown dramatically in Latin America and I think that rather than compete with this phenomenon the Roman Catholic Church must dialogue with *los Pentecostales*. Both must participate in joint ecumenical dialogue. Such an alternative leads to a pneumatological perspective of God as the giver of symbols and visions. He is the one who stirs up the prophetic call to work for justice in the midst of the poor, marginalized, and oppressed.

A common critique of the usage of *mestizaje* is the lack of inclusion of diverse contexts. For example, Manuel Vásquez, Miguel De La Torre, and Néstor Medina strongly critique the appropriation of *mestizaje* because it was used as a nation building metanarrative that systematically destroyed any semblance of otherness. Such critique is a major reason these authors preferred more inclusive terminologies such as *mestizajes*, *mestizaje*-intermixture, or world traveling hybridity. These seek to acknowledge intra-Latin@ tensions as well as alternate dimensions of Latin America that arise from an analyis of *mestizaje*. The trend is to parse and explore the web of relationality that characterizes Latinos in the US and to build bridges from a common colonial past.

Hibridez

These concerns ultimately call for a more nuanced theology and for a greater degree of inter-Latino dialogue and understanding. I also think they describe genuine calls for the examination of *mestizaje*-intermixture which I see as a concern for *hibridez*. Above, I appealed to Vásquez's use of hybridity in order to discuss a Latin American or Latino *hibridez*. I argue that *hibridez* reveals the tension of the self and the other or what I call *identidad* and *otredad*. It also speaks of the dynamic between *identidad* and *otredad*. This dynamic is embedded from the origins of Latin America and qualifies the way identities emerge or are constructed. It is a dynamic and interplay qualified by different *encuentros*, *reencuentros*, *encontronazos*, and *desencuentros*.

Again, these terms emphasize relationship and the desire to build a just mutuality or relationality. The values of *amistad, fraternidad, hermandad,* and *hospitalidad* move *hibridez* in the direction of a just relationality. Through the work of the Spirit these may move towards a posture of healing between individuals and communities that exist together in contrast and competition. Such examples are the rich and poor, the haves and have-nots, the undocumented immigrant and the full citizen.

Hybridity and *Hibridez*

Because of this strong concern for the other I decided to pursue a Latino *hibridez* informed by discussions on postcolonial hybridity. I do not absorb the term uncritically. These two exist in similar tensions yet are different and independent. We notice that there are *variedades* of hybridities emerging from different contexts and these must be discussed. So our discussion on *hibridez* leads us to discover intra-Latino tensions as well as tensions going in directions outside the Latino community towards other *variedades*.

I am not doing away with *mestizaje*. I think that the Latino theological community must continue to engage *mestizaje* because it gives *hibridez* a necessary historical grounding. *Mestizaje* grounds us in *lo cotidiano.* And again, I note that I do not merely translate the term hybridity to Spanish. I have qualified it with *mestizaje* and as such is based on Latin American realities and *lo cotidiano.* Using *hibridez* leads us to consider *otredad* and *identidad* within *mestizaje.* It also leads us to consider *identidad* and *otredad* outside of *mestizaje* such as *mulatez,* Amerindian realities, Caucasians, African Americans, etc. *Hibridez* allows us to observe and nuance *encuentros, reencuentros, encontronazos* and *desencuentros* that characterize the people of Latin America. *Hibridez* becomes an identity marker as well as a methodology for an intercultural dialogue. Again, this is what I think Medina hinted at through *mestizajes* and *mestizaje*-intermixture.

To understand the process of relationality I dialogued with Bhabha's hybridity to gain perspective on the interstitial space that leads to interpretations and reinterpretations of dominant discourses by those on the margins of power. A look at Bhabha's theory on hybridity allows us to engage and further nuance the cultural exchanges and discover the different meanings that arise from cross-cultural dialogue. We can also nuance forms of resistance that characterize those on the margins of society. This allows us to understand the subversive action of crossing a border without the proper documentation. Bhabha is but one *variedad* of hybridity with which we may dialogue.

I repeat this last thought on *hibridez*. If we embrace it, then we must remain grounded in *lo cotidiano*. We must not escape the reality of the suffering people of Latin America or the visceral reality of the working urban poor in the US. *Lo cotidiano* is an essential element in building a just Latino theology precisely because it includes the poor. Moreover, *hibridez* cannot become a closed scientific system with a closed and rigid scientific worldview. We must allow for a dimension informed by God's immanent and transcendent Spirit active in *lo cotidiano* if we are to make use of *hibridez*. It is through this inclusion of God's Spirit in *lo cotidiano* that I make a return to theology through *hibridez*.

Hibridez leads us to explore *indocumentados* who make the journey *al norte*. We become sensitive to situations arising from *lo cotidiano* and *re-presentaciones híbridas*, like the way they interpret the American Dream, and chronic poverty that chokes the life out of the poor. We strive to include these experiences in our theological constructs.

Hibridez and Religious Symbols

In my return to theology I followed the example that many Latino authors make by focusing on popular religion and the symbols of the community. I gave an analysis of *mestizaje* and its role in interpreting *la Virgen de Guadalupe* and *Jesucristo*. God identifies with those on the margins of society and the *pueblos híbridos latinoamericanos*. God's identification through Jesus Christ is redemptive and transformative. *La Virgen de Guadalupe* is a powerful prophetic pneumatological symbol that affirmed the emerging *cosmovisión* of the vanquished Aztecs. In *Jesucristo*, we have the Savior of the world who lived, worked, and ministered among those of society. His work also included those beyond his own people, the gentiles. He even identified with immigrants who now enter the United States' backdoor through scorching deserts and rivers as a *mojado* (wetback) in Egypt.

I also analyzed a particular author that captured interests of *hibridez* in *Sor Juana Inés de la Cruz*. In many ways she is a precursor to liberation theologies. Her particular use of the *Loa al Divino Narciso* reflects an *híbrida* consciousness that reconciled both Amerindian and European *cosmovisiones*. We can only wonder how much more she could have written if those in power had not censured her. She shows us that the language of *hibridez* moves beyond simplistic either-or categories to those who are both-and, and a-little-bit-of-this-and-a-little-bit-of-that – much more inclusive categories.

An *híbrida* vantage point from a Pentecostal perspective also reveals layers of a popular pneumatology. Some authors described the *Virgen de Guadalupe* as a pneumatologically inspired symbol in that the Holy Spirit is present in hybrid locations and hybrid realities. This is also a bridge to Pentecostalism. Because most literature for the Latino community comes from the Roman Catholic perspective I wanted to make an ecumenical step and examine what *hibridez* may look like as arising from *lo cotidiano* in a Pentecostal perspective. In order to open *identidad* to *otredad* I analyze the work of the Spirit. The Spirit decenters *identidad* to allow *otredad* the opportunity for dialogue.

For these reasons I examined the Azusa Street revival. I think Azusa Street is a place that allows us to see the discomfort and *encuentros* of early Pentecostals and how the Spirit of God was at work here. Azusa Street could have potentially been a vignette into *hibridez* as a liminal reality where the Holy Spirit enters the lives of the marginalized and oppressed of society. However, it was more of a disillusionment and a disappointment because this gestalt for theological reflection remained stagnant. Azusa did not change the dynamics of paternalism present in Pentecostal mission.

I also described Azusa Street because it is a place many North American Pentecostals refer to in order to describe their theology and I wanted to highlight that it was a place where some undocumented immigrants were present, in this way tainting a pristine place. I also want to make it clear that it was not the only place where it was so, as the Southwest experienced a transnationalism from below where immigrants crossed the border between the US and Mexico in many other ways. From Azusa I also use the terminology *evangélico* because this terminology builds bridges to right wing evangelicals in the US who do not understand (or wish to understand) the phenomenon of undocumented immigration. I examined *pentecostales* in order to establish that Latin@s were also present in the Azusa Street revival and to propose theories of what they experienced through *hibridez* in the power of the Spirit. I also look at the revival because many Pentecostals seem to have sanitized the rawness of Azusa Street. The Spirit was at work in a place of *encontronazos* as in the example from the Indian from the central part of Mexico who was an active participant in the revival.

It is possible to see that undocumented immigrants have been a part of the Pentecostal heritage and an evangelical heritage. Daniel Ramírez describes a *de facto* hospitality and a very ambiguous border in which people from both sides of the border crossed into each other's countries. Such movements characterize Christianity in the Southwestern US.[3]

Consequently, I wanted to present an emerging pneumatological *hibridez* and what this seemed to do or could have potentially done for the participants who happened to be Latino and/or immigrants. There are testimonies written down in Spanish in the Azusa Street papers, as well as descriptions of Amerindian Mexicans participating alongside the English-speaking people in the revival.

My conclusion is that Azusa Street demonstrated much promise to rearticulate pneumatologically ecclesiological constructs in an image of the Kingdom of God. The Spirit actively embraced, transformed, and empowered individuals and communities across cultural and socioeconomic divides. However, this potentiality remained unused energy or wasted potential. Perhaps it was too radical for the people at Azusa Street. Sánchez-Walsh critiques that we may question just how free these people were during and especially after the revival. The evidence is that we may have murdered the Spirit of God with our cultural divides, ecclesiological constructs, and paternalistic models of mission resulting from the revival. This is a *desencuentro*. Perhaps revisiting the revival and considering what the Spirit was doing may help us reconstruct our ecclesiologies and our conceptions of *otredad*. The Spirit's work must reorient our affections and praxis in order to produce a theology of hospitality.

---

[3] See the article by Daniel Ramírez, 'Call Me "Bitter"'.

Hibridez and Visions from *Lo Cotidiano*

In order to build such a theology, I made my own turn to *lo cotidiano*. I wanted to examine one of the most marginal experiences in North American society, undocumented immigration. I interviewed undocumented immigrants who were members of *iglesias evangélicas* in the US. The reason I interviewed them was to gain a sense of their *hibridez* and of their experience on the margins of society.

Most of those I interviewed earned below minimum wage. Some have worked twelve hours or more per day without overtime pay. The reason they never reported this was that they did not want to lose their jobs. José, who I also mentioned in the previous chapter, worked 12-14 hours per day 7 days a week and never got a single cent of overtime pay. This is a common thread for many of these workers. I have met *jornaleros* of different nationalities who sometimes did a day's or a week's worth of work for contractors who abandoned them at the side of the road rather than pay them. This leads to conditions of a constant angst where the temptation for many is to self-medicate with drugs such as marijuana and alcohol. Some of the people I interviewed experienced severe depression. A man named Jairo, for example, led a life of drunkenness and intoxication until he found salvation in a Pentecostal church. This is *lo cotidiano*. This is the place where our theological reflection arises.

In the midst of the complexity of their situation Christianity was their source of support. The Holy Spirit affirmed their humanity. In their congregations they felt at home in an alien land. The church became a place for tears, miracles, and groans too deep for words. The worship service was a place of hope that affirmed that they are made in God's image. They experienced the immanence of God's Spirit through conviction, regeneration, sanctification, healing, miracles, and tongues despite their social location. This same Holy Spirit birthed new *visiones* in their lives that ultimately altered *cosmovisiones* and gave rise to a new sense of personhood. He was present through charismatic empowerment and manifestations in order to help them survive in a context that had been antagonistic to them. Despite cultural differences the Spirit affirmed them in their *otredad* and brought them to a place where they could begin to develop just relationships with their North American peers.

For example, Isaura mentioned how she dropped out of school and how her boyfriend abandoned her when she was pregnant at sixteen years of age. She was jobless and completely down and out. However in the midst of her anguish, torment, and sin the church became a place of refuge for her. Rather than being condemned she found God in the most hopeless moment. She felt God's conviction and accepted Jesus as her Lord and Savior. Later, she received the Baptism of the Spirit so that her life became a vessel to be used in the life of the church. When she received the baptism of the Spirit she prayed in tongues for her whole family and for her entire church. She became an unlikely prophet and mouthpiece of God. She now has an outlook of hope when there once was hopelessness. This is an example of the reconstruction of life at the most basic human level that happens in the ghettos of North America through the power of the Holy Spirit.

Pneumatology

It is here that I propose that such realities cannot allow for a pneumatology focused on an ethereal symbolic presence; rather, pneumatology should be explored in light of *hibridez*. A Latino theology must engage the Spirit's work in *lo cotidiano*. A unique contribution of Pentecostal theology is a theology of the Holy Spirit that contributes to the commitment to work among the marginalized and oppressed of society. The Spirit decenters our *identidad* and keeps our drives of totalization in check. The Spirit demonstrates his care for the poor, including people who are marginalized by the *encontronazos* and *desencuentros* of *hibridez*.

For *Pentecostales*, pneumatology develops in action and praxis. The pastor (many times the pastor is female) is a person of action seldom having adequate time to study. Similarly, their implicit theology is a theology of action. For example, in the New Testament the Spirit is associated with action, being the finger of God (Lk. 11.20). This is a metaphor that implies action. The programmatic statement of Jesus in Luke also gives programmatic markers for the work of the Spirit (Lk. 4.18-20) in which the Spirit moves Jesus to action, in Mark the Spirit impelled Jesus to the wilderness. Paul uses the words indicating action when speaking about the workings of the Spirit in the lives of Christians. *Charismaton, diakonion, energematon, energon, phanerosis* are all words involving some kind of action by the Spirit of God (1 Corinthians 12). Whenever we see the Spirit in the New Testament it involves *energon* and *phaneron*. The Spirit cannot remain removed from *lo cotidiano*. He fills it. The Spirit is not a static being far removed from the concrete social context. Rather he is God in action in context.

The Holy Spirit dwells in the interstitial space and liminal realities in *hibridez* moving humanity to participate in God's work in the threshold and tensions between *identidad* and *otredad*. We must remember that this interstitial space is a place of creativity or destruction. It may be positive or negative. It may affirm identity or it may diffuse identity. It may create an *encuentro* that moves us to mutual understanding or a *desencuentro* resulting in adverse fallout.

For example, identity for immigrants is negotiated in liminal spaces. María, whom we met in the previous chapter, worked a marginal job for subpar wages. However, she did not let this stop her from participating and engaging in this society. She became conscious of the fact that she is a child of God. She became an important part of her congregation by supporting it and the people in it through many means. Another woman, Petra, became an intercessor in her church. She believes that she changes history through prayer. She also believes the Holy Spirit has empowered her to be a witness no matter where she goes. Although she cleaned houses for a living she was able to pray for one of these homeowners and God healed him. It is reminiscent of the slave girl that told Naaman about the prophet in Samaria (2 Kgs 5.1-4). This girl was a marginal person in society but nonetheless reached out to one of the most powerful persons in the empire.

In this interstitial space of *encuentros* the Spirit is at work bringing people to the knowledge of God. He brings them to salvation, reorients humanity's affections, and sanctifies them so they may build relationality between *identidad* and *otredad* oriented after God's orthopathos and His Kingdom. The Spirit also gives life altering and life affirming *visiones* through emerging prophetic symbols and the charismata. As we have taken note it may be through a powerful symbol or a vision like *la Virgen de Guadalupe*. In the case of Pentecostals, it may be through the powerful experience of Spirit baptism. The Spirit is *fons vivus, ignis, caritas*. Human experiences with the Spirit of God provide powerful cathartic elements for transformation and empowerment. In Isaura's case she spoke in tongues throughout the night and prophesied over the people in her congregation. She had a powerful experience where the Spirit radically changed her life.

We can state that in the language of *hibridez* that the immanent Spirit decenters *identidad* and orients it towards a just mutuality with *otredad*. It is this God-consciousness, or Spirit consciousness, that begins a process of reorienting human life. The Spirit forms, shapes, and acts upon the human subject *concienzándolos*, transforming them, and sanctifying them. Yet this immanence is in tension with a divine *otredad*. *Otredad* is tied to the transcendence of God. This transcendence indicates that God is still holy other. With this tension with transcendence one avoids domesticating the Spirit or making the Spirit a mere spirit (lowercase). Furthermore, the Spirit decenters us through his immanence and calls us towards *otredad* precisely because he is God who immanently enters into relationship with us as ultimate holy *otredad* and transcendence. God's action in the world is one where he draws near, but simultaneously reminds us how holy, special, and distinct he is. In this, God acts upon the human world to move it towards his purposes.

This demonstrates a relationship between two dimensions of the Spirit that remain in tension. He is immanent. However, the Spirit also transcends humanity. We are ultimate *otredad* to him. This ultimate otherness or transcendence requires a relationship to him because he cannot be domesticated or sanitized. God's radical identification in the work of the Spirit serves as a call for alignment to the will of God and to yield to the Spirit in sanctification. He draws near and identifies with humanity. He feels humanity's pain. He identifies and empathizes with humanity. This immanence also reminds us that holiness and sanctification are not unattainable. This immanent-transcendent tension is important in the formation of a pneumatological conscientization.

This tension gives us an orthopathic model for us to follow in our relationship to God and as a consequence it influences interpersonal relationships. We are brothers and sisters in Christ. God gives us a new citizenship. His Kingdom calls us to a different order of life in which we move towards each other loving one another. Likewise, we leave space for the transcendence of the other in in order to establish a just mutuality where we value the other's development and integrity.

Tensions Revealed by the Spirit

Theologically, this is a great paradox. God is transcendent holy other to humanity yet he is relational, close, and immanent to humanity. Daniel Castelo, for example, holds this tension together by stating that God is so distant from the world's occurrences that his presence carries meaning and significance.[4] Through his immanence he identifies with us and draws us towards him. Through his transcendence he reveals that he is greater than human suffering. His immanence reveals that he loves us, yet through his transcendence we are not equal to him and that we must navigate our relationship with him with fear and trembling (Phil. 2.12). This transcendence also provides the ground of transformation in humanity. It is a source of *theosis* or sanctification. As God draws us to right relationship to him he makes us aware of our own *otredad* and draws us into right relationship to him. This has positive consequences for our relationship to our neighbors.

The very condition of experiencing the Spirit of God has several redemptive dimensions. In *Jesucristo*, God makes a kenotic movement through which we experience redemptive qualities of God's action in the world today. Simultaneously, we may also experience redemptive dimensions through a similar kenotic work by the Holy Spirit in entering the human sphere in *lo cotidiano*. This is an implicit tension between transcendence and immanence that is highlighted by Pentecostals all around the world because God has not abandoned his creation.

Immanence

I explore more about the immanence of God as experienced by Pentecostals and their experience with the Spirit in order to inform this pneumatology. The Spirit as *fons vivus* begins the spiritual pilgrimage when he pours out God's *caritas* in our lives. This love becomes the source, motive, and power of living in the Spirit.[5] Spirit baptism and tongues, in particular, provide an experience with the immanent God. In our language of *hibridez* the Spirit moves in pol-

---

[4] Daniel Castelo, *The Apathetic God: Exploring the Contemporary Relevance of Divine Impassibility* (Eugene, OR: Wipf and Stock Publishers. 2009), pp. 14-15.

[5] García-Johnson, *The Mestizo/a Community of the Spirit*, p. 77.

yphonic and polyglot ways that make God's deeds of power meaningful to the hearers as a polyphonic experience of intersubjective nature.[6] What appears as intersubjective difference that is confusing and non-intelligible requires a referral to the jurisdiction of the Holy Spirit.[7]

In this move of entering the human sphere, the Spirit decenters human *identidad* and draws it to God's holy *otredad*. He reveals his holy *identidad* that embraces our broken *otredad*. Since God has emptied himself and drawn nigh to humanity, his call for his people is to move in community oriented towards reconciliation – first with his holy *otredad* present in our midst, and second with the *otredad* of our neighbors, regardless of language, race, or creed.[8] This includes social location, documented or undocumented status for immigrants in the US. The Spirit's work of identification is powerful and reveals God's grace. However, the work of the Spirit does not stop at mere identification. God's work engages in *theosis* or sanctification. God's work results in humanity engaging in his work on earth by producing an experience where we are aware of our intersubjective difference yet move towards each other for the social good.

I am speaking of sanctification on several planes. In Spanish, for example, the language of sanctification is not relegated to mere spiritual terms where the Christian community's role is to become mere moralizers. To be righteous before God is to be *justo*, or just. To yearn for righteousness is to yearn for *justicia* or justice. In a hybrid heteroglossic voice this term simultaneously carries both personal connotations for righteousness *and* political/social connotations for justice. Here the individual looks to God's holiness and otherness but does not remain in an isolated spiritual freak show state of absolute moral purity. The individual moves to weep and act for his or her people, nation, neighbors, the poor, widow, orphan, alien, immigrant, and others on the margins of society. The divine enters the world of the poor, undocumented, and reviled. In the case of María, Isaura, José, and Silvia we see that God pours his love out in their hearts and they move towards right relationality with him and with their fellow human beings, regardless of social

---

[6] García-Johnson, *The Mestizo/a Community of the Spirit*, p. 77.

[7] García-Johnson, *The Mestizo/a Community of the Spirit*, p. 77.

[8] García-Johnson, *The Mestizo/a Community of the Spirit*, p. 80.

location. The Spirit moves us to establish a just relationality, including social outcasts.

Transcendence

There are some few concerns for immanence in light of the work of Daniel Castelo. I wish to acknowledge these concerns and see how these serve a model of *hibridez* in light of *identidad* and *otredad*. Castelo warns us that the transcendence of the Spirit is a necessary dimension that must be coupled together with his immanence.[9] I think that it is a dimension of God's relationality that mirrors that of *otredad* in *hibridez*. An emphasis on God's *otredad* in transcendence invites us to proper relationality. For example, an outside force does not affect God's will.[10] He is not caught by surprise at our actions. Neither does God's immanence collapse into creation. Consequently, we are not pantheistic. Neither is a charismatic experience with the Spirit used to justify an individual's or a community's whims. For example, Pentecostal circles are infamous for saying things like, 'God told me so'. Fleeting feelings are attributed to God. A healthy view of transcendence relates to his otherness and that his will is separate and distinct from humanity.

I hold this in tension with God's immanence as a powerful redemptive dimension that must be recovered in theology. Castelo also strives to maintain God as an impassible co-sufferer that does not collapse God into the world.[11] Jesus and the Spirit suffer; and as Castelo states, this is an act of solidarity that is hopeful, redemptive, and glorifies God's love for Creation.

His transcendence also moves us to a different way of life – God's holiness, and one oriented after his Kingdom. God sanctifies humanity by calling us towards this transcendence where humans live according to a Kingdom not of this world. He invites us to holy relationships sanctified in him. This in turn, allows us to make analogous connections towards *otredad*. Again, it is a tension that preserves a high view of both his immanence and his *otredad*.

Mayra Rivera, for example, states that transcendence serves as a way to model interpersonal and intercultural interaction for it is a

---

[9] Castelo, *The Apathetic God*, p. 39.

[10] Castelo, *The Apathetic God*, p. 16.

[11] Castelo, *The Apathetic God*, pp. 138-39.

mirror of the relation between God and human beings.[12] It allows us to maintain reverence and respect for the other. She also states that many theologies emphasize one or the other, transcendence or immanence.[13] For example, on the one hand, she states that liberation theology places too much emphasis on the immanence of God also impoverishing our ideas of holiness, morality, *otredad*, and interpersonal relationships.[14] On the other hand, she critiques radical orthodoxy as placing too much emphasis on the transcendence of God.[15] This creates problems for theology and consequently for interpersonal relationships. These reflect distancing, coldness, and a lack of social commitment.

For Rivera, divine transcendence is necessary to assure God is God.[16] God cannot be reduced to a finite knowable being. However, carried to its extreme, an over-emphasis on transcendence suspends embodied life, self-expression, sexuality, aesthetic experience, and human political communities. Rivera states that a proper view of divine transcendence upholds the relative worth of creatures.[17] This suspension is a double-edged sword. It can cause us to devalue our earthly conditions, but it can also cause us to uphold their relative worth over-against nothingness.[18] God's transcendence must be balanced with the immanence of God. But the caution is that an over emphasis on immanence tends to reduce God and his creation to something that can be fully grasped by human constructs or reduced to categories within social systems.[19]

In this manner this balance between transcendence and immanence moves humanity to participate in God and carry a relationship with God. We open up to that which is beyond ourselves through a movement of identification and differentiation present in *identidad* and *otredad*. In light of *hibridez*, we open up beyond our own *identidad* to move towards God's *Otredad* and our neighbors' *otredad*. The orientation of creation's development towards God

---

[12] Mayra Rivera, *The Touch of Transcendence* (Louisville: Westminster John Knox Press, 2007), p. 19.

[13] Rivera, *The Touch of Transcendence*, p. 19.

[14] Rivera, *The Touch of Transcendence*, p. 19.

[15] Rivera, *The Touch of Transcendence*, p. 19.

[16] Rivera, *The Touch of Transcendence*, p. 19.

[17] Rivera, *The Touch of Transcendence*, p. 19.

[18] Rivera, *The Touch of Transcendence*, p. 19.

[19] Rivera, *The Touch of Transcendence*, p. 37.

comes from what lies beyond itself. This is ultimately God and his divine nature. He moves us towards his heteroglossic *justicia* that includes social directions towards/with fellow human beings regardless of what may differentiate us. The openness to others promotes a self-critique and avoids self-absolutization.[20] I suggest that the Holy Spirit and the experience of Pentecost are also valuable resources to discuss *identidad* and *otredad* in light of the Spirit's immanence and transcendence.

Spirit Baptism

The Baptism of the Spirit is an event par excellence demonstrating the theological tension between immanence and transcendence.[21] Naturally, this is similar to the tensions in *hibridez* of *identidad* and *otredad*. Humans are located in the created visible while God is Holy Other and transcendent.[22] However, God does his work in us as we experience the transcendent God through his immanent Spirit.[23] This is a tension that serves as a model to engage *otredad* because God is immanent to the human world yet infinitely transcendent and holy other.

The Pentecost event in Acts 2 reveals the nature of the Christian community as one of continuous emergence, diversity, and heterogeneity.[24] The Spirit divine and holy other enters into the life of the community identifying with them and empowering them. Yet the community is ever mindful of the Spirit's transcendence. In the midst of this diversity God calls us to a different social ethic. Through this experience the Spirit God empowers the church to live a cruciform relationality and simultaneously levels all human positioning on social ladders. The community of the Spirit must be a communal transformational place in and through which God's Spirit continues to transform our unredeemed culture.[25] The Holy Spirit helps our discussion of *hibridez* in that the church may become a community of the Spirit shaped by an ecclesiological para-

---

[20] Rivera, The Touch of Transcendence, p. 37.
[21] García-Johnson, *The Mestizo/a Community of the Spirit*, p. 95.
[22] García-Johnson, *The Mestizo/a Community of the Spirit*, p. 95.
[23] García-Johnson, *The Mestizo/a Community of the Spirit*, p. 95.
[24] García-Johnson, *The Mestizo/a Community of the Spirit*, p. 97.
[25] García-Johnson, *The Mestizo/a Community of the Spirit*, p. 97.

digm capable of embracing the heterogeneity and fluidity of cultural life and the inventive powers of God's Spirit.[26]

These are concepts that may help us give voice to pneumatological concerns as it pertains to *Pentecostales* and ultimately *liberación*. In heteroglossic hybrid voice the issue of *liberación* for *evangélic@s* is intimately tied to the internal and external freedoms that the Spirit brings to individuals and communities and the orthopathic qualities that lead to orthopraxis. God brings a new life marked by freedom from vices, sin, spiritual oppression, and moral injustice. Simultaneously, God brings about his Kingdom marked by liberation from political injustice, social oppression, structures of sin, and social injustice.

The Baptism of the Spirit is also a doorway to experience new *visiones* and the building of new *cosmovisiones* for the community of faith. This is the case of undocumented persons in church. Through the experience of the Spirit they experience new *visiones*. God reveals new realities for the ones on the fringes of the community. This *visión* is not only an ecstatic image or picture, but also a life-altering archetype upon which to model life in the future. God presents his people with a new alternative to their present predicament. For example, Isaura, despite being a single mom, became God's prophet. She was also presented with a new reality and a new dimension in which to live. She was no longer condemned but became a part of the community. Her life took on a new sense of value through a *visión* birthed by God.

Such a *visión* is not only a mental image but it is the ability to think about the future differently and with hope. *Dios nos da un futuro preferido* (God gives us a preferred or preferable future). Again, it is not only a transcendental state or an ecstatic mystical experience but a new life firmly rooted in *lo cotidiano* as an alternative to the way things are. Isaura is no longer cut off, cast off, or ostracized. Instead, she is now a citizen of a different kingdom and lives according to that kingdom. Her life is full of potentiality that will make a difference. God is on her side. She has an altered *cosmovisión*. She is made in his likeness and will do her best to make the most out of her current predicament.

---

[26] García-Johnson, *The Mestizo/a Community of the Spirit*, p. 97.

A Final Interplay: God's Pathos and Immutability

One last tension that pneumatology leads us to consider is God's passion and immutability. Samuel Soliván's *The Spirit, Pathos, and Liberation* is significant to understand a Pentecostal perspective of the work of the Spirit. His understanding is that God is intimately present in the community of faith. I must state at this point that some theologians, like Daniel Castelo, are concerned with the direction that Soliván takes his readers particularly as it relates to the impassibility of God.[27] I suggest that the impassibility of God and the passibility of God must be maintained in tension. All language is anthropomorphic and in a certain sense is limited in the way it depicts God because it uses human elements to describe God. Furthermore, God is not capricious or volatile. He does not act out of his passion without restraint or self-control. While Soliván's ideas are valuable we cannot do away with the doctrine of the impassibility of God. Nonetheless, I now describe God's pathos, or passibility.

Empathy, Pathos, Passibility

The importance of this orthopathos is that the Holy Spirit reveals that God is not apathetic; rather, he is deeply involved in human affairs.[28] Soliván's understanding of the pathos of God is rooted in the Old Testament Prophets. He states that these reveal that God has shared with us the expression of passion.[29] Furthermore, God is touched and moved by our brokenness.[30] God also joins the struggle of the poor, marginalized, and oppressed. Elaine Padilla's doctoral dissertation also describes this passionate God.[31] It is a matter of profound interest in the Latino community to talk about God's Spirit as God's pathos, his immanence, and his identification with Creation. For example, Padilla also maintains that the Hebrew *ruach* is an onomatopoeic word that strongly denotes passion.[32]

The discussion on *orthopathos* is related to his immanence. It allows these authors to recover a sense of God's solidarity with the

---

[27] Daniel Castelo, 'A Crisis in God-talk? The Bible and Theophany', *Theology* 105.858 (2007), pp. 411-16.

[28] Samuel Soliván, *The Spirit, Pathos and Liberation* (JPTSup 14; Sheffield: Sheffield Academic Press, 1998), pp. 50-52.

[29] Soliván, *The Spirit, Pathos and Liberation*, p. 56.

[30] Soliván, *The Spirit, Pathos and Liberation*, p. 60.

[31] Elaine Padilla, *Passionate God* (PhD, Drew University, 2011), pp. 83-84.

[32] Padilla, *Passionate God*, p. 83.

poor, marginalized, and oppressed.[33] In this manner, the suffering of the poor becomes a resource for liberation as it relates to the Latino community in the US.[34] Soliván states: 'orthopathos is that insight, that self-understanding which infuses in the oppressed the strength to rise above the dehumanization of their daily conditions'.[35] Jesus had an orthopathic consciousness informed by the Holy Spirit. This is key in the pneumatological turn that we are making.

Furthermore, the Holy Spirit transforms the victim and their circumstance in a liberative move. For Soliván, God moves away from *apatheia* towards involvement with the created order. He calls humanity to move from apathy to liberation because of the presence of the Holy Spirit. First, the Spirit is in the world and in us; he is immanent. Second, the Spirit produces faith as knowledge that is both cognitive and affective.[36] It is through the Spirit that God corrects a bifurcation between reason and experience and the tendency to remain in apathy towards suffering. In light of what has preceded us it is through *encuentros* that the Spirit reorients sin through the gestalt of orthopathos in the lives of individuals and communities. This orthopathos directly relates to the heteroglossic sanctification of humanity.

The work of the Spirit of God invites us to see them in a new way. They are fellow citizens of a different kingdom. They are people that have been touched by the finger of God. They are fellow human beings who have experienced the gracing of the Holy Spirit and who experience a new citizenship not limited by human borders.

Orthopathos works to liberate the marginalized not just through indignation with the way things are but through a transformative experience with the Spirit of God that leads to tangible action. Again, this is a heteroglossic perspective on the concept of *liberación*. I make this point again. In *liberación* the Spirit inspires and is present in the individual through charismatic manifestations. The individual experiences spiritual freedom and is set free from his or her personal bondages, chains, the demonic, sin, and self-destructive

---

[33] Soliván, *The Spirit, Pathos and Liberation*, p. 60.
[34] Soliván, *The Spirit, Pathos and Liberation*, p. 61.
[35] Soliván, *The Spirit, Pathos and Liberation*, p. 62.
[36] Soliván, *The Spirit, Pathos and Liberation*, p. 62.

behavior. Simultaneously, *liberación* carries strong political dimensions of freedom. Communally, the Spirit moves believers towards the work of justice through engagement with social structures and communities.

In this move, the work of the Spirit is not reduced to a narcissistic individualism; on the contrary, the Spirit pushes towards community life with inter/multi-cultural *convivencia* of the Holy Spirit. Simultaneously rather than wallow in personal sin or perpetuate the structures of sin, the individual and the community of faith are oriented to right relationality towards both God and neighbor. In *lo cotidiano* the Spirit moves the community of faith towards mercy and a heteroglossic *liberación*. This dimension creates a new pathos oriented towards life in the Kingdom of God and a new *cosmovisión*.

This orthopathos is informed by other sources: the Scriptures, Christian tradition, socio-economic *conscientización*, family relations, and the personal experiences of the sufferers.[37] The Holy Spirit is not relegated exclusively to an ethereal, unearthly, or phantasmagorical quality; neither does the Spirit refer to the mere sense of the Latin, *animus*, spirit or attitude. Rather, the Spirit is the very Person of the relational God who is involved in inspiring and creating alternate *visiones* and *cosmovisiones* in the context of the visceral reality and *lo cotidiano* of the poor, marginalized, and oppressed.

Tensions with Immutability/Impassibility

Again, Castelo gives several reasons why theology should preserve a sense of pathos/passibility along with immutability/impassibility, even when it has become popular to value the passibility and pathos of God in contemporary theology and practice.[38] Castelo's warning is interesting as he is a Latino Pentecostal theologian, like Soliván. But one of the dangers that Castelo points out is that God becomes a mere human projection.[39] He also states that if God is subject to the same things as humans, the conclusion is that he is not divine.[40] Castelo proposes that we preserve God's orthopathos and immutability in what he calls theopathos.[41]

---

[37] Soliván, *The Spirit, Pathos and Liberation*, p. 62.
[38] Castelo, 'A Crisis in God-talk? The Bible and Theophany', p. 412.
[39] Castelo, 'A Crisis in God-talk? The Bible and Theophany', p. 412
[40] Castelo, 'A Crisis in God-talk? The Bible and Theophany', p. 413.
[41] Castelo, 'A Crisis in God-talk? The Bible and Theophany', p. 413.

In his view, God is the source of all things, including emotions.[42] Castelo is able to balance out this pathos without collapsing back into an *apatheia* that is insensitive to the suffering of the world, such as undocumented immigrants and those going through injustice. Another concern to preserve the impassibility of God is that a God who is characterized as simply and only like us is a God who is a fellow victim to the fallen condition of the world.[43] Similar to my concern for transcendence, God does not collapse into sin or a sinful state for, 'if God suffers as we do what hope do we have then? If God is not beyond our immediate trials, what recourse do we have'?[44] Through Christ and through the Spirit, God enters the human story. He is the Paraclete, God with us. Yet the fact that he is still holy other gives us a resource for empowerment in the Spirit. He suffered as we have, but has the ability to move and empower us beyond suffering. He gives humanity a new identity and purpose. He also empowers and transforms humanity.

Castelo also states that the Jewish mindset was more preoccupied with questions of interrelatedness and relationship rather than what things are ontologically in themselves.[45] This is the tension one sees with Pentecostal communities of the Spirit. God relates to us and only through that relationship can we know him as he is. These tensions do not let theology and practice stagnate. Rather they call us creatively forward to transformation, holiness, and social justice. Transcendence and immanence are held together paradoxically in an elegant manner.[46]

Orthopathos and *la Manera de Ser*

Through the Spirit individuals are now subjects of history and they are also God's voice, feet, and hands in the world. The Holy Spirit guides us to a deep conscientization and reorientation in an affective dimension that is intimately personal, but is profoundly related to social transformation. Pneumatological emphasis may help us recover important theological motifs in a discussion of *hibridez*. The Spirit orients us to right *ciudadanía*, and a *desarrollo ético personal*

---

[42] Castelo, 'A Crisis in God-talk? The Bible and Theophany', p. 413.
[43] Castelo, 'A Crisis in God-talk? The Bible and Theophany', p. 414.
[44] Castelo, 'A Crisis in God-talk? The Bible and Theophany', p. 414.
[45] Castelo, 'A Crisis in God-talk? The Bible and Theophany', p. 414.
[46] Castelo, 'A Crisis in God-talk? The Bible and Theophany', p. 416.

verdadero.[47] These two dimensions are new *visiones* that reorient their *cosmovisiones*.

Ciudadanía

This idea of citizenship is also related to our discussion of *hibridez*. *Mestizo* and *mulato* people have been non-citizens, and they experience alienation in several ways. In some cases, the alienation is so severe that they are perceived as non-human or as completely irreconcilable Other.[48] However, God gives the marginalized and oppressed true citizenship. As a citizen, each person is valuable in the eyes of God. He or she may contribute as an active participant in the community.

Citizenship is a repeated motif throughout the New Testament as there was a dynamic interplay between Jewishness versus Romanness, or citizens versus aliens. This interplay has orthopathic implications for the church. It is in this context that Paul describes how the Spirit bestows true citizenship. Paul writes to the Ephesians exhorting that believers have access to God the Father in Christ through the Spirit (Eph. 2.18-19). Immediately afterwards, he tells his readers that it is this what makes them full citizens in his Kingdom. Consequently, this idea of a new citizenship takes on political implications in light of the suffering and injustices that these people suffer as non-citizens or as marginalized people in the Roman Empire. Through a liberative move, the Spirit bestows true citizenship, regardless of their citizenship status to the powers that be on earth. These new citizens are also active subjects of history, not just mere objects of history. Through an *encuentro* with the Holy Other God the people of faith are made citizens and part of the family of God. Despite their earthly citizenship or identity and the characteristics of that culture and take on a new citizenship or identity and a new culture, or a new *identidad* in light of God's *otredad* that moves towards a just *hibridez* with God and others.

This theological motif also describes a reorientation to citizenship. This means that individuals exist in a tension between the

---

[47] Darío López, *Pentecostalismo y Transformación Social* (Buenos Aires: Kairós, 2000), p. 13.

[48] Marisol De La Cadena, '¿Son mestizos los híbridos? Las políticas conceptuales de las identidades andinas', *Unversitas Humanística* 61 (January 2006), pp. 51-84 (p. 54). Her analysis is particularly helpful because she talks about the non-citizenship of *mestiz@* peoples in Perú.

Kingdom of God and that of earthly kingdoms. Their communities must engage society establishing the Kingdom of God in their contexts. For example, North American Christians must strive to make sense not only of their undocumented brothers and sisters, but also of Christians from around the world. Our denominational structures must acknowledge the international church and that there are people gifted of the Spirit and are capable of leadership outside any one specific country. Through the Spirit the marginalized and oppressed are made subjects of history in contrast to being non-persons and aliens. In the community of faith, they experience the dignity of being recognized as persons created in the image of God.

Citizenship is also related to some of the deepest human affections. Citizenship often goes together with patriotism and in some cases ethnocentrism and racism. The experience of the Spirit reorients the individual and the community's understanding of citizenship. Their new citizenship means they are stewards of their earthly societies. This carries an idea of social responsibility and civic duty for they will have to give an account of their earthly conduct. Rather than lead to escapism it should lead them to engage oppressive structures of society.

In many ways undocumented immigrants in the church call us to re-evaluate and redefine our notions of Christian citizenship. [49] There is a necessary alienation by which individuals learn to find and narrate their lives within the broader history of the Church and the Bible. Daniel Castelo thinks that the fact that undocumented immigrants are foreigners in society and at the same time foreigners in the world depict two kinds of alienation that produce a picture of the Christian life that is a portrayal of what it means to be a member of God's coming Kingdom. [50]

This double alienation produces a Christian life ever mindful of where true Christian citizenship lies. It is not disengaged from action on earth but more conscious of the importance of establishing the Kingdom of God on earth. It leads to a radical disengagement with jingoist sentiments and to one that is concerned for the work

---

[49] Daniel Castelo, 'Resident and Illegal Aliens', *Apuntes* 23.2 (Summer, 2003), pp. 65-77.

[50] Castelo, 'Resident and Illegal Aliens', p. 66.

of God on earth. We live in a tension between earthly kingdoms and the coming Kingdom. We are still responsible for what happens here and it is in tension with the new life that is to come.

This is the case of the individuals I have interviewed. They know where their true citizenship lies. Whether they are deported or whether an amnesty is passed they will continue to live for God. In this way their churches function as communities of affirmation and as communities of resistance. Where no one cared for them, these individuals found acceptance in the church. They live in a holy space where they may move and live freely despite society's restrictions.

Desarrollo Ético Personal Verdadero

Lastly, I point to social transformation of individuals and communities. Darío López states, 'Los proyectos [Pentecostales] tienen como horizonte la transformación integral de las relaciones humanas y del contexto familiar y social de las personas involucradas en estos espacios de la dignidad humana'.[51] These are places for the affirmation of a new citizenship in the power of the Spirit where 'se afirma, promueve y defiende la dignidad intrínsica de todos los seres humanos como creación de Dios'.[52]

This authentic personal ethical development is related to a model of sanctification that leaves room for a crisis experience with the Spirit of God and one that is open to the therapeutic work of the same Spirit. Again, individuals are now subjects of history and they are also God's voice, feet, and hands in the world. The Spirit works to bring about a deep conscientization and reorientation in affective dimensions that are intimately personal but are also profoundly related to social transformation.

I believe a reason that *Pentecostales* have not written prolifically about this is that their constituency is mainly the poor of society. As such, they do not have the opportunities to write or discuss their theology. The aberrations we see such as the prosperity gospel are really a much smaller portion of their thought than what they get

---

[51] López, *Pentecostalismo y Transformación Social*, p. 25. 'Pentecostal projects have as their horizon the integral tranformation of human relationships and of the family and social context of the person involved in the space of human dignity'.

[52] López, *Pentecostalismo y Transformación Social*, p. 28. 'The intrinsic dignity of all human beings as the creation of God is affirmed, promoted, and defended'.

credit for. Unfortunately, those who adhere to such aberrations usually have much more presence in the media and other forms of communication.

Conclusion

This final chapter has been a theological expression of undocumented immigration and the work of the Holy Spirit in liminal spaces through *hibridez*. In many ways it has been birthed out of my direct experiences with these people and as a practitioner involved in their lives. I believe that many Pentecostals have wanted to study and write about their communities but very few have ever had the opportunity. My concern has been to understand their location and their faith theologically. I have entered a world full of contradictions and where it is not easy to exist and have tried to make sense of what I have observed in light of theology.

In writing about theology I have made an entry point through *mestizaje*. The reason I chose *mestizaje* is that Latino theologians describe it as the *locus theologicus* of this community. The most important contribution of *mestizaje* is that it helps us to gain a historical grounding and the contextualization of this theology. Nonetheless, *mestizaje* has experienced some very poignant critiques. This is the reason I decided to see how we can expand its understanding through *lo cotidiano* and through various critiques such as Medina's *mestizaje*-intermixture. I also made us aware that the perspective that dominates *mestizaje* is a Roman Catholic perspective.

In a way to continue expanding and building theology I wished to include *Pentecostales*, *catrachos*, and *indocumentados* into theology. One thing I did to allow for even more inclusion is to explore a world-traveling hybridity. I did this in order to see how a dialogue with an emerging *hibridez* expands our understanding of mestizaje. *Hibridez* allows us to see a dynamic of *identidad*, *otredad*, and different *encuentros*. This allows for an analysis of the web of relationality that characterizes Latinos. In this analysis my one caution is that *hibridez* must remain grounded in *mestizaje*'s *lo cotidiano*.

In light of this *hibridez* I explored the religious symbols of the community. I studied Azusa Street to understand a multicultural work of the Holy Spirit. I also interviewed Honduran immigrants in order to understand their predicament and their particular understanding of their faith. In this chapter it is important to notice the convergence of *mestizaje, lo cotidiano, hibridez, la fe pentecostal,* and *inmigrantes indocumentados.*

In light of theology an examination of *hibridez* must lead us to mutual understanding and proper relationality. God enters the liminal or interstitial spaces that are places of affirmation or destruction through the Holy Spirit. This is a theology that takes God's presence in *lo cotidiano* seriously. God is interested in accomplishing humanity's salvation, justification, liberation, and sanctification. This Holy Other God confronts humanity's sins, both personal and social. God manifests himself in humanity with the charismatic life in the Holy Spirit and reorders humanity through his orthopathos.

The Spirit affirms the person, whatever their location may be in society. Whether they are *mestizo, híbridos,* or *zambo,* they experience God's sanctifying force and participate in God's work. They are made citizens of his Kingdom even if they have no citizenship on earth. From our previous reflections on Azusa Street, we understand Seymour's vision of love ordered by the Spirit as the plumb line for Christian community. The Spirit is at work within the individual, but also beyond the individual.

The Spirit calls us to redirect our idolatry towards power, its symbols, and structures. He calls us to a renewed *cosmovisión.* In order to balance out the Spirit's immanence we look at the Spirit's transcendence. His transcendence leads us to cleanse our unholy lust for power, our unholy tongues, and our disordered desire. The Holy Spirit questions our motives for social structuring and the way these have been formed. The tension of *identidad* and *otredad* also bring questions of God's immanence and transcendence to the forefront. This is a tension that is maintained by the Spirit and corrects idolatrous drives towards totalization in light of the other.

A pneumatological perspective using *hibridez* must include solidarity with the poor, marginalized, and oppressed. It must also actively engage with society and work for the transformation of society through heteroglossic *liberación* and *justicia.* The Holy Spirit reorients humanity by calling it to God's orthopathos. This orthopathos moves in a direction of social transformation for their communities and societies precisely because of the work of the Spirit.

The implication of the work of the Holy Spirit is embedded with sociopolitical and religious significance. The inclusion of a pneumatic perspective reveals the work of God as the empowering immanent and transcendent God that continues to stand in solidarity with the poor, marginalized, and oppressed, including the alien and hopelessly other. He works for *justicia* for the *liberación* of humanity. God takes us on a relational journey of *hibridez* through the Spirit's immanence and transcendence correcting our social positioning through a pneumatologically inspired orthopathos.

APPENDIX A: METHODOLOGICAL PROCESS

I am not a trained ethnographer. But I tried to remain as faithful as possible to the principles of ethnography. I cannot say I was detached from the issue because I am a pastor in New York and have seen the struggles of immigrants first-hand. So I had a vested interest in presenting the life of those who had entered the US without proper inspection. My interest in the issue also stems from experience. I have pastored two churches where I have dealt directly with people who were present without inspection in the US. I have also lived transnationally as a missionary kid. So this transnational movement across borders through immigration is of great interest to me.

It was fairly easy to establish a rapport with the people I interviewed. I am fluent in Spanish and know the nuances of Honduran culture and humor. Hondurans are generally friendly if you are nice to them and they like to talk about their experiences and reminisce about their home country. I also tried to establish credibility with those with whom I had a formal interview. They wondered why I was interested in them, but I kindly explained that I was a student and wanted to learn more about their experience in the US. Overall, they were very eager to tell their stories. If I had taken the time to get to know them, it was not difficult to sit down over a cup of coffee and ask questions about their life experiences. In fact, on a couple of occasions I hardly asked any questions.

My main strategy for gathering information was conducting interviews, both formal and informal. Although pastoring in New York, I am also a participant observer of people in my congregation who had no documentation entering the US. Many times I interacted with these people in the street, at their jobs, or in their homes. I live in their neighborhoods and visit stores and places where they work. Sometimes getting to know them was as simple as striking up a conversation at a restaurant with a waiter or waitress and learning more about them.

I held many informal interviews with several people. Once, I interviewed the owner of a barbershop where I had a haircut. On another occasion I took someone to have a cup of coffee and asked some questions relating to their experiences. They freely shared, ultimately sharing their reasons for leaving their home country and the reasons they are in the US. Many times I gained a sense of their documented or undocumented status through phrases they would say, like 'I wish I had papers in this country'.

I also conducted formal interviews of a few people who freely volunteered this information. For the interviews included in this book I changed the names of those whom I interviewed in order to protect their anonymity in light of their undocumented status. I also guaranteed them I would not reveal their names. Overall, formal interviews were my least preferred method of gathering research because interviewees were a little apprehensive if I had a recording device or a notebook. Nonetheless, I had to take notes in order to get a sense of what was important to them, and I also used a recording device. Appendix B is a sample of questions that I asked. These were formal interviews where I sat down with a recording device, and/or notebook in order to take notes.

APPENDIX B: QUESTIONS THE AUTHOR ASKED DURING INTERVIEWS

What is your name?
How are you?
So tell me, how long have you lived in the US?
Where are you from?
What was life like in your *pueblo*?
Did you like it?
What did you do for a living in your home country?
Why did you decide to leave?
How old were you when you left?
Did you have family in the US?
Was it easy to come to the US?
Did you adjust easily to life in the US?
What kind of jobs have you had?
How does earning a living in your home country compare to earning a living in the US?
Do you have any family in your home country?
Do you send your family money?
What would you tell someone who wants to come to the US?
How has your faith helped you in your journey to the US and in adjusting to life here?
Are you a Christian?
Are you involved in church?
Has the church played a major role in your life?
Where do you go to church?
How do you serve God in your church?
What are your future plans now that you are here in the US?
Do you want to return to your home country?
How have you tried to survive here in the US?
If they told the author they had entered the US without inspection:
What was your experience crossing the border like?
Did people help you?
Did people try to harm you?

What route did you take?
Did you travel with company?
Did you pray during your journey?
Where did you stay?
How was your experience?

BIBLIOGRAPHY

Álvarez, Miguel, *Integral Mission in Contemporary Perspective: A Model for the Pentecostal Churches with Special Reference to Honduras* (PhD; Oxford: Oxford Centre for Missions Studies, 2013).

Álvarez, Miguel, David Ramírez, and Raúl Zaldivar, *El Rostro Hispano de Jesús* (Elgin, IL: Editorial Universidad para Líderes, 2009).

Anderson, Thomas P, *Politics in Central America: Guatemala, El Salvador, Honduras and Nicaragua* (New York: Praeger, 1988).

Andrade Coelho, Ruy Galvao, *Los Negros Caribes de Honduras* (Tegucigalpa, Honduras: Editorial Guaymuras, 1981).

Annese, John M, 'Taking Back the Streets of Port Richmond', Staten Island Advance. http://www.silive.com/news/index.ssf/2010/07/tak ing_back_the_streets_of_por.html. Accessed October 11, 2010.

Aponte, Edwin David, and Miguel A. De La Torre (eds.), *Handbook of Latina/o Theologies* (St. Louis: Chalice Press, 2006).

Aquino, María Pilar, *Our Cry for Life: Feminist Theology from Latin America* (Maryknoll, NY: Orbis Books, 1993).

'August 11th', *The Apostolic Faith* 1.1 (September, 1906), p. 3.

Augustine, *The Confessions of Saint Augustine* (trans. Carolinne White; Sacred Wisdom Series; London: Frances Lincoln Publishers, 2001).

—*On the Spirit and the Letter* (trans. William John Sparrow-Simpson; Society for Promoting Christian Knowledge, 1925).

Bañuelas, Arturo (ed.), *Mestizo Christianity: Christianity from Latino Perspective* (Maryknoll, NY: Orbis Books, 1995).

Bartleman, Frank, *Azusa Street* (Plainfield: Logos International, 1980).

Bau, Ignatius, *This Ground is Holy* (New York: Paulinist Press, 1985).

Bean, Frank D., Barry Edmonston, and Jeffrey S. Passel (eds.), *Undocumented Migration to the US: IRCA and the Experience of the 1980's* (Washington, DC: Urban Institute Press, 1990).

Benjamin, Medea, *Don't Be Afraid Gringo* (New York: Harper & Row, 1989).

Benôit Monin and Kieran O'Conner, 'Reactions to Defiant Deviants: Deliverance or Defensiveness?', in Jolanda Jetten and Matthey J. Hornsey (eds.), *Groups: Dissent, Deviance, Difference, and Defiance* (Oxford: Wiley Blackwell, 2011), pp. 117-34.

Bentley, Jeffrey, 'Honduras', in Melvin Ember and Carol Ember (eds.), *Countries and Their Cultures* (2 vols.; New York: Macmillan Reference, 2001), pp. 979-90.

Bhabha, Homi K, *The Location of Culture* (London: Routledge, 2004).

Bridges Johns, Cheryl, *Pentecostal Formation: A Pedagogy Among the Oppressed* (JPTSup 2; Sheffield: Sheffield Academic Press, 1993).

Brown, Robert McAfee, *Gustavo Gutierrez: An Introduction to Liberation Theology* (Maryknoll, NY: Orbis Books, 1990).

Carroll R., M. Daniel, *Christians at the Border* (Grand Rapids: Baker Academic Press, 2008).

Cashmore, Ernest (ed.), *Encyclopedia of Race and Ethnic Studies* (New York: Routledge, 2004).

Castelo, Daniel, *The Apathetic God: Exploring the Contemporary Relevance of Divine Impassibility* (London: Paternoster, 2009).

—'A Crisis in God-talk? The Bible and Theophany', *Theology* 110.858 (2007), pp. 411-16.

—'Resident and Illegal Aliens', *Apuntes* 23.2 (Summer 2003), pp. 65-77.

Cerna, Mario, 'Los Deportados en Honduras Sumaron 46 mil en 2010', *El Heraldo* http://www.elheraldo.hn/Ediciones/2010/12/24/Noticias/ Deportados-en-Honduras-sumaron-46-mil-en-2010. Accessed December 24, 2010.

Chanady, Amaryll, 'La Hibridez como Significación Imaginaria', *Revista de Crítica Literaria Latinoamericana* 24.49. (1999), pp. 265-79.

Chávez, Eduardo, *Our Lady of Guadalupe and Saint Juan Diego: The Historical Evidence* (Lanham: Rowman and Littlefield, 2006).

Cohen, Robert, *Global Diasporas: An Introduction* (New York: Routledge, 2008).

Corbett, Jim, *Goatwalking* (New York: Viking Penguin, 1991).

Crespo, Orlando, *Being Latino in Christ* (Downers Grove: Intervarsity Press, 2003).

De La Cadena, Marisol, '¿Son mestizos los híbridos? Las políticas conceptuales de las identidades andinas', *Unversitas Humanística* 61. (January 2006), pp. 51-84.

De La Torre, Miguel A. and Gastón Espinosa (eds.), *Rethinking Latino(a) Religion and Identity* (Cleveland: Pilgrim Press, 2006).

De La Torre, Miguel A. and Miguel Aponte (eds.), *Handbook of Latino Theologies* (Duluth: Chalice Press, 2006).

Department of Social Sciences, University of California San Diego, *Nican Mopohua* (1649) http://weber.ucsd.edu/~dkjordan/nahuatl/nican/ NicanMopohua.html. Accessed September 29, 2011.

Departamento 19, 'Migrantes Hondureños en los Ojos de los Carteles', http://departamento19.hn/index.php/portada/69/6859.html. Accessed August 14, 2012.

Diario La Prensa, 'María Otero: Ponerle fin a al impunidad es clave', http://www.laprensa.hn/Secciones-Principales/Honduras/Tegucigal pa/Maria-Otero-Ponerle-fin-a-la-impunidad-es-clave#.UFdIX0LffEU. Accessed Sept. 14, 2012.

—'La Violencia Ha Dejado 46,450 Muertos en Honduras en los Últimos Once Años', http://www.elheraldo.hn/Secciones-Principales/Al-Fren te/La-violencia-ha-dejado-46-450-muertos-en-Honduras-en-los-ultimo s-once-anos. Accessed March 12, 2012.

—'Honduras Continúa en la Lista Negra de EUA en Tránsito Ilícito de Droga', http://www.laprensa.hn/Secciones-Principales/Honduras/Te gucigalpa/Honduras-continua-en-lista-negra-de-EUA-en-transito-de-d rogas-ilicitas#.UFdHskLffEU. Accesseded Sept. 14, 2012.

Donadoni, Chiara and Eugenia Houvenaghel, 'La Hibridez de la tradición judeocristiana como reivinidicación del sincretismo religioso de la nueva España: El divino narciso de Sor Juana', *Neophilologus* 94 (2010), pp. 459-75.

Dudley, William (ed.), *Immigration: Opposing Viewpoints* (San Diego: Greenhaven Press, 2002).

Elizondo, Virgilio, *The Future is Mestizo* (Boulder: University Press of Colorado, 2000).

—*Galilean Journey: The Mexican–American Promise* (Maryknoll, NY: Orbis Books, 2000).

—'Mestizaje as a Locus of Theological Reflection', in Arturo Bañuelas (ed.), *Mestizo Christianity: Theology from the Latino Perspective* (Maryknoll, NY: Orbis Books, 1995), pp. 7-27.

Elizondo, Virgilio (ed.), *The Treasure of Guadalupe* (Lanham, MD: Rowman and Littlefield, 2006).

Ellingwood, Ken, *Hard Line: Life and Death on the U.S.-Mexico Border* (New York: Vintage Books, 2005).

England, Sarah, 'Negotiating Race and Place in the Garifuna Diaspora: Identity Formation and Transnational Grassroots Politics in New York City and Honduras', *Identities* 6.1 (1999), pp. 5-53.

Espín, Orlando, 'Immigration, Territory, and Globalization: Theological Reflections', *Journal of Hispanic Latino Theology* 7.3 (2000), pp. 46-59.

—'Mary in Latino/a Catholicism: Four Types of Devotion', *New Theology Review* 23.3 (August 2010), pp. 16-25.

Espín, Orlando and Miguel H. Díaz (eds.), *From the Heart of Our People: Latino/a Explorations in Catholic Systematic Theology* (Maryknoll, NY: Orbis Books, 1999).

Espinosa, Gastón, 'Brown Moses: Francisco Olazábal and Mexican–American Pentecostal Healing in the Borderlands', in Gastón Espinosa and Mario García (eds.), *Mexican–American Religions: Spirituality, Activism and Culture* (Durham, NC: Duke University Press, 2008), pp. 263-95.

—'"El Azteca": Francisco Olazábal and Latino Pentecostal Charisma, Power, and Healing in the Borderlands', *Journal of the American Academy of Religion* 67.3 (September 1999) pp. 597-616.

—'The Holy Ghost is Here on Earth: The Latino Contributions to the Azusa Street Revival', *Enrichment Journal* 11.2 (Spring 2006), pp. 118-25.

Flores, Barbara Anne Therese, *Religious Education and Theological Praxis in Context of Colonization: Garífuna Spirituality as a Means of Resistance* (PhD, Northwestern University, 2001).

Francis, Samuel T, *The Sanctuary Movement: Smuggling Revolution* (Monterey: American Immigration Control Foundation, 1986).

García Canclini, Néstor, 'Culturas Híbridas y estrategias comunicacionales', *Estudios sobre las culturas contemporáneas* 3.5. (June 1997), pp. 109-128.

—*Hybrid Cultures: Strategies for Entering and Leaving Modernity* (Minneapolis: University of Minnesota Press, 1995).

García-Johnson, Oscar, *The Mestizo/a Community of the Spirit: A Postmodern Latino/a Ecclesiology* (Eugene: Pickwick Publications, 2009).

Girad, René, *I See Satan Fall Like Lightning* (Maryknoll, NY: Orbis, Books, 2002).

—*The Scapegoat* (Baltimore: John Hopkins University Press, 1986).

Goizueta, Roberto, *Caminemos con Jesús: Towards a Hispanic/Latino Theology of Accompaniment* (Maryknoll, NY: Orbis Books, 1995).

González, Justo, *Santa Biblia: Reading the Bible Through Hispanic Eyes* (Nashville: Abingdon Press, 1996).

González, Michelle, *Sor Juana: Beauty and Justice in the Americas* (Maryknoll, NY: Orbis Books, 2003).

—'Who is Americana/o?', in Catherine Keller, Michael Nausner, and Mayra Rivera (eds.) *Post Colonial Theologies* (St. Louis: Chalice Press, 2004), pp. 58-78.

Gracia, Jorge J.E, 'Ethnic Labels and Philosophy: The Case of Latin American Philosophy', in Eduardo Mendieta (ed.), *Latin American Philosophy, Currents, Issues, Debates* (Bloomington, IN: Indiana University Press, 2003), pp. 124-49.

Groody, Daniel and Gioachinno Champese (eds.), *A Promised Land, A Perilous Journey* (Notre Dame: University of Notre Dame Press, 2008).

Guillermoprieto, Alma, *The Heart that Bleeds: Latin America Now* (New York: First Vintage Books, 1995).

Gutierrez, Gustavo, *The God of Life* (Maryknoll, NY: Orbis Books, 1991).

—*A Theology of Liberation* (Maryknoll, NY: Orbis Books, 1973).

Harris, Andrew and Laurence Viele Davidson, 'Rights Groups Say Alabama Immigration Laws Should Stay on Hold', *Bloomberg Business Week*, http://www.businessweek.com/news/2011-09-30/rights-groups-say-alabama-immigration-laws-should-stay-on-hold.html. Accessed October 1, 2011.

Hiddleston, Jane, *Understanding Movements in Modern Thought: Understanding Postcolonialism* (Durham: Acumen, 2009).

Hoefer, Michael, Nancy Rytina, and Bryan C. Baker, *Population Estimates* (Department of Homeland Security, Office of Immigration Statistics), January 2010. http://www.dhs.gov/xlibrary/assets/statistics/publications/ois_ill_ pe_2009.pdf. Accessed December 12, 2010.

Holden, Robert, *Armies Without Nations: Public Violence and State Formation in Central America 1821–1960* (New York: Oxford University Press, 2004).

'Identificadas 31 Victimas de Masacre en Tamaulipas', *Terra*. http://www.terra.com.mx/noticias/articulo/948152/Identificadas+31+victimas+de+masacre+en+Tamaulipas.htm. Accessed August 26, 2010.

Iglesia de Dios del Perú, 'Declaración del Trabajo del I Encuentro Nacional de Líderes Juveniles sobre los Derechos Humanos: La defensa de la vida' (August 30, 1998).

Isasi-Díaz, Ana Maria, *En la Lucha: In the Struggle* (Minneapolis: Fortress Press, 1993).

—*Mujerista Theology: A Theology for the Twenty-First Century* (Maryknoll, NY: Orbis Books, 1996).

Johnson, Maxwell E., *The Virgin of Guadalupe: Theological Reflections of an Anglo-Lutheran Linguist* (Lanham, MD: Rowman and Littlefield, 2002).

Johnson, Paul Christopher, 'On Leaving and Joining Africanness Through Religion: The "Black Caribs" Across Multiple Diasporic Horizons', *Journal of Religion in Africa* 37 (2007), pp. 174-211.

Keller, Catherine, *et al.* (eds), *Postcolonial Theologies: Divinity and Empire* (St. Lous: Chalice Press, 2004).

La Prensa, 'Hay Medio Millón de Hondureños Secuestrados por Maras', http://www.laprensa.hn/Secciones-Principales/Honduras/Apertura/Hay-medio-millon-de-hondurenos-secuestrados-por-maras. Accessed May 7, 2013.

—'La Guerra Volvió a Chamelecón', http://www.laprensa.hn/Secciones-Principales/Honduras/Apertura/La-guerra-volvio-a-Chamelecon-las-maras-rompen-la-tregua La Prensa. Accessed May 7, 2013.

Lee, Jung Young, *Marginality: The Key to Multicultural Theology* (Minneapolis: Fortress Press, 1995).

Levinson, David and Melvin Ember (eds.), *American Immigrant Cultures: Builders of a Nation* (2 vols.; New York: Simon and Schuster Macmillan, 1977).

Lopez, Abundio, 'Spanish Receive the Pentecost', *The Apostolic Faith* 1.2 (October, 1906), p. 4.

López, Darío, *La Misión Libertadora de Jesús* (Lima, Perú: Ediciones Puma, 2004).

—*Pentecostalismo y Transformación Social* (Buenos Aires, Argentina: Ediciones Kairós, 2000).

López, Mark Hugo, and Ana González Barrera, 'Salvadorans May Replace Cubans as Third-Largest Hispanic Group', *Pew Research Center* http://www.pewresearch.org/fact-tank/2013/06/19/salvadorans-may–soon-replace-cubans-as-third-largest-u-s-hispanic-group/. Accessed June 9, 2013.

Martínez, Luz Ángela, 'La Celda, El Hábito, y la Evasión Epistolar en Sor Juana Inés de la Cruz', *Revista Chilena de Literatura* 81 (2012), pp. 69-89.

McDougal, Christopher, *Born to Run* (New York: Doubleday Press, 2009).

Medea, Benjamin, *Don't be Afraid Gringo* (New York: Harper & Row, 1989).

Medina, Nestor, *Mestizaje: Mapping Race, Culture and Faith in Latina/o Catholicism* (Maryknoll, NY: Orbis Books, 2009).

Mendieta, Eduardo (ed.), *Latin American Philosophy, Currents, Issues, Debates* (Bloomington: Indiana University Press, 2003).

New York Times, 'City of Endangered Languages', http://video.nytimes.com/video/2010/04/28/nyregion/1247467719180/city-of-endangered-languages.html. Accessed May 5, 2010.

Nican Mopohua (1649) http://weber.ucsd.edu/~dkjordan/nahuatl/nican/NicanMopohua.html. Accessed September 29, 2011.

Ngai, Mae M, *Impossible Subjects: Illegal Aliens and the Making of Modern America* (Princeton: Princeton University Press, 2004).

Padilla, Elaine, *Passionate God* (PhD, Drew University, 2011).

Peters, María, 'Hondureñas Se Convierten en Esclavas Sexuales en Mexico', http://www.elheraldo.hn/Secciones-Principales/Al-Frente/Hondurenas-esclavas-sexuales-en-Mexico. Accessed September 3, 2012.

Powell, Lisa D, 'Sor Juana's Critique of Theological Arrogance' *Journal of Feminist Studies in Religion* 27.2 (2011), pp. 11-30.

Prabhu, Anjal, *Hybridity: Limits, Transformations, Prospects* (Albany: SUNY Press, 2007).

Purcell, L. Edward, *Immigration: Opposing Viewpoints* (Phoenix: Oryx Press, 1995).

Ramírez, Daniel, 'Borderlands Praxis: The Immigrant Experience in Latino Pentecostal Churches', *Journal of the American Academy of Religion* 67.3 (September 1999), pp. 574-89.

—'Call Me "Bitter"': Life and Death in the Diasporic Borderland and the Challenges/Opportunities for Norteamericano Churches', *Perspectivas* 11 (Fall 2007), pp. 39-66.

—*Migrating Faith: Pentecostalism in the United States and Mexico in the Twentieth Century* (Chapel Hill: UNC Press, 2015).

Recinos, Harold J, *Good News from the Barrio: Prophetic Witness for the Church* (Louisville: Westminster John Knox Press, 2006).

—Hear the Cry! A Latino Pastor Challenges the Church (Louisville: Westminster John Knox Press, 1989).

Rivas, Ramón D., *Pueblos Indigenas y Garífuna de Honduras* (Tegucigalpa, Honduras: Editorial Guaymuras, 2004).

Rivera Rodríguez, Luis R., 'Immigration and the Bible: Comments by a Diasporic Theologian', *Perspectivas* 10 (Fall 2006), pp. 23-36.

Rivera, Mayra, *The Touch of Transcendence* (Louisville: Westminster John Knox Press, 2007).

Robeck, Mel, *The Azusa Street Mission and Revival: The Birth of the Global Pentecostal Movement* (Nashville: Thomas Nelson, 2006).

Rodríguez, Daniel A, 'No Longer Foreigners and Aliens: Toward a Missiological Christology for Hispanics in the United States', *Missiology* 31.1 (January 2003), pp. 51-67.

Rodríguez, Jeanette, *Our Lady of Guadalupe: Faith and Empowerment Among Mexican–American Women* (Austin: University of Texas Press, 2001).

Rokus, Brian, 'No Murder Conviction in Mexican Immigrant's Beating Death', http://articles.cnn.com/2009-05-01/justice/pa.immigrant.beating_1_death-of-luis-ramirez-ethnic-intimidation-charges-juvenile?_s= PM:CRIME. Accessed May 1, 2009.

Sánchez, Daniel R, *Hispanic Realities Impacting America* (Fort Worth: Church Starting Network, 2006).

Sánchez Walsh, Arlene, *Latino Pentecostal Identity: Evangelical Faith, Self, and Society* (New York: Columbia University Press, 2003).

Sandoval, Edgar and Jonathan Lemire, 'Mexican Community in Staten Island Wary after Wave of Crimes', *New York Daily News*, http://www.nydailynews.com/ny_local/2010/09/26/2010-09-26_under_attack_mexicans_in_si_wary_after_wave_of_hate_assaults.html. Accessed October 11, 2010.

'The Same Old Way,' *The Apostolic Faith* 1.1 (September, 1906), p. 3.

Saulny, Susan, 'Black? White? Asian? More Young Americans Choose All of the Above', *The New York Times* (January 30, 2011). http://www.nytimes.com/2011/01/30/us/30mixed.html?ref=us. Accessed January 30, 2011.

Schwaller, John Frederick, *The History of the Catholic Church in Latin America: From Conquest to Revolution and Beyond* (New York: New York University Press, 2011).

Smilde, David, *Reason to Believe: Cultural Agency in Latin American Evangelicalism* (Berkeley: University of California Press, 2007).

Smith, James K.A., *Thinking in Tongues: Pentecostal Contributions to Christian Philosophy* (Grand Rapids: Eerdmans, 2010).

Soliván, Samuel, *The Spirit, Pathos, and Liberation* (JPTSup 14; Sheffield: Sheffield Academic Press, 1998).

Sobrino, Jon, *Jesus the Liberator* (Maryknoll, NY: Orbis Books, 1999).

Sorens, Matthew and Jenny Hwang, *Welcoming the Stranger* (Downers Grove: InterVarsity Press, 2009).

Spencer, Nick, *Asylum and Immigration: A Christian Perspective on a Polarised Debate* (Cambridge: Paternoster Press, 2004).

Stabb, Martin, *In Quest of Identity* (Chapel Hill: The University of North Carolina Press, 1967).

State of Arizona, Senate Bill 1070, http://www.azleg.gov/legtext/49leg/2r/bills/sb1070s.pdf. Accessed January 12, 2011.

Stonequist, Everett V., *The Marginal Man: A Study in Personality and Cultural Conflict* (New York: Russell and Russell, 1961).

Swain, Liz. 'Garifuna Americans', in Rudolph J. Vecoli, *et al.* (eds.), *Gale Encyclopedia of Multicultural America* (vol. 1; Detroit: Gale Cenage, 2000), pp. 686-97.

Taylor, Charles, 'The Politics of Recognition', *Multiculturalism* (Princeton: Princeton University Press, 1994).

Taylor, Paul, *et al.*, 'When Labels Don't Fit: Hispanics and Their Views of Identity', http://www.pewhispanic.org/2012/04/04/when-labels-dont-fit-hispanics-and-their-views-of-identity/. Accessed April 4, 2012.

United Nations Office on Drugs and Crime, 'Global Study on Homicide 2011: Trends, Contexts, Data', http://www.unodc.org/documents/data-and-analysis/statistics/Homicide/Globa_study_on_homicide_2011_web.pdf. Accessed January, 2012.

US Census Bureau, 'Hispanics in the US', http://www.census.gov/population/www/socdemo/hispanic/hispanic_pop_presentation.html. Accessed November 30, 2009.

—'Population by Sex, Age, Hispanic Origin, and Race: 2008', http://www.census.gov/population/www/socdemo/hispanic/cps2008.html. Accessed November, 30, 2009.

Vásquez, Manuel A., 'Rethinking Mestizaje', in Miguel A. de la Torre and Gastón Espinosa (eds.), *Rethinking Latino(a) Religion and Identity* (Cleveland: Pilgrim Press, 2006), pp. 129-60.

Vera, Fortinio Hipólito, *Informaciones sobre la Milagrosa Aparición de la Santísima Virgen de Guadalupe Recibidas en 1666 y 1723* (Imprenta Católica a Cargo de Jorge Sigüenza, 1889).

Vigil, Ángel, *The Eagle on the Cactus* (Englewood: Greenwood Publishers, 2000).

Villafañe, Eldin, *The Liberating Spirit: Toward an Hispanic American Social Ethic* (Grand Rapids: Eerdmans, 1993).

Wink, Walter, *The Powers That Be* (New York: Galilee Publishing, 1999).

Weir, Robert (ed.), *Class in America* (2 vols.; Westport: Greenwood Press, 2007).

Yong, Amos, 'The Im/Migrant Spirit: De/Constructing a Pentecostal Theology of Migration', in Peter C. Phan and Elaine Padilla (eds), *Theology and Migration in World Christianity: Contextual Perspectives* (2 vols; New York: Palgrave Macmillan, 2013), II, pp. 133-53.

Yugar, Theresa Ann, *Sor Juana Inés de la Cruz: Feminist Reconstruction of Biography and Text* (PhD, Claremont Graduate University, 2012).

Index of Biblical References

Index of Names

CPSIA information can be obtained
at www.ICGtesting.com
Printed in the USA
LVHW051733110522
718483LV00010B/553

9 781935 931591